'Michael Williams is a ca
intelligent man with an e1
of humour. He makes a
his wife, Dani, pastor On

'This reflects in the writing of this wonderful book, *Dying to Get There*. Michael gently helps us navigate the less-talked-about subject of the afterlife and cleverly helps us think about how that affects us today. He meticulously researches the relevant Bible passages, joining the dots and drawing out some eye-opening gems.

'I know heaven will be bigger, brighter, better than we can possibly imagine, but this book has certainly whetted my appetite.'
Simon Jarvis, Senior Leader of the One Church Network

'Like a great teacher, Michael breaks this huge subject down for me so I can understand and be inspired.'
Mark Ritchie, Evangelist

'Thanks, Michael, for listening to the Spirit. Your motivational gifts of teaching and exhortation are both evident in this thoughtful, analytical, Scripture-based, and thoroughly enjoyable treatise. You have created an atmosphere of encouragement about our incredible *there*, allowing us to make Spirit-informed decisions and practical applications *here*. Well done!'
Mark Middleton, Executive Director, Equip Canada

'My clients have various reactions to the idea of death – fear being the most common. Just the word 'death' or 'dying' can be enough to send some into panic. Even confirmed atheists who believe in nothing after death often have secret fears about death that are incongruent with their stated beliefs. Whether you are a believer or a non-believer, the biggest amplifier of fear is avoidance.

'This is just one of the reasons I love Michael's book; thinking about death with hope (and humour) helps us to live better in the here and now, without either obsessing about it or denying it. If you are scared of death, read this book. If you are scared of being scared of death, read it. If you're trying not to think about death, read it. If you are looking forward to death, read it. Face death and really live!'

Deborah Laxton, Clinical Lead, Hope Psychological Services CIC

Dying to Get There

A vision of heaven to transform our lives on earth

Michael Williams

instant
apostle

First published in Great Britain in 2021

Instant Apostle
104 The Drive
Rickmansworth
Herts
WD3 4DU

British Library Cataloguing-in-Publication Data

A catalogue record for this book is available from the British Library.

This book and all other Instant Apostle books are available from Instant Apostle:

Website: www.instantapostle.com

Email: info@instantapostle.com

ISBN 978-1-912726-54-7

Printed in Great Britain.

For Jackson, my son, His child

Contents

Introduction

The great blessing of every Christian is the ability to see the future with a life-changing hope.

The message of Jesus means that we can be optimistic in every circumstance and view death without fear. What lies on the other side of that curtain is a priceless inheritance worth getting excited about. Its value is not less than *here*, but so much more that it cannot be counted in comparison. The effect of this hope on the early disciples is unmistakable. They lost any notion that *here* would satisfy and displayed extraordinary enthusiasm about being *there* with Jesus. There is no doubt this hope fuelled their boldness in preaching the good news, and their courage in the face of persecution, even to death.

My personal experience in pastoral ministry has brought me to the conclusion that this expectancy is far from common now when it should be a benefit of every Christ follower. We have the equivalent of a billion pounds in the Bank of Hope but live with a pocket-change-sized perspective of the future, and the present is poorer for it.

Many Christians lack understanding about what is in store for them *there*. The fear of death still runs like an open smartphone app in the back of our minds, and when faced with loss, many suffer doubt in God's character and existence. The impact of this gap in our understanding can show up in our mental and spiritual health.

It's time to add to our revelation of the cross, the revelation of the resurrection. It's time to break free from the ropes of fearfulness, and step into the 'confident hope'[1] of eternal life.

If you are reading this book and still on a journey towards faith in Jesus, I pray this will help concrete your decision to trust in Him. Because when we start to grasp what's in store for us, just like those early followers of Jesus, we'll be dying to get *there*.

Michael Williams
Summer 2021

---

[1] Colossians 1:5.

Our faithless world tells us
we have everything to fear
and everything to lose. But
our hope in Christ reminds
us we have absolutely
nothing to fear and
everything to look forward to.

1
Dying To Get There

But Stephen, full of the Holy Spirit, gazed
steadily into heaven and saw the glory of God,
and he saw Jesus standing in the place of honor
at God's right hand.
Acts 7:55

I once heard a story about a lady who died during a church service.

Now, my wife will tell you that I've put a few to sleep during my sermons, but I'm yet to bore anyone to death, as far as we know. What's memorable about this story is the way in which the lady left *here* for *there*.

The first thing you should know is that it seems this lady had a friendship with Jesus spanning decades. This was no religious exercise. She knew Him so closely that she was *different*. You know the kind of Christian I mean? While elderly, her joy and her faith were infectious. She had found Jesus when she was a young woman and successfully cultivated a friendship with Him, resulting in a pretty full experience of life. Both the young and old

15

loved to be near this lady to catch her faith and feel the love.

Second, the church service was buzzing. Not one of those solemn, quiet services. This was like a rock concert in comparison. After a half hour or so of singing her heart out in the front row of church, she sat down next to her best friend, leaned into her and whispered the words, 'Isn't Jesus lovely?' and beamed. Before her friend could respond, this lady's eyes had closed, and moments later she had left.

Her body was still on the front row, but she was somewhere else, almost definitely singing.

Many Christians may consider the benefits of death during the announcements slot in a church service, but for this lady, it was not boredom that led to her promotion from one worship service into another. No, she was excited, full of the Holy Spirit, revelling in His presence, assured, peaceful and smiling.

There's another guy who left *here* for *there* with a smile, but it wasn't in a church service. In fact, quite the opposite. In Acts 7 we read that Stephen was surrounded by a gang of radicals with rocks in their hands and a hatred enflamed by his insistence that they, the religious elite, were unfaithful to God. He was on trial for his faith in Jesus and had used the opportunity to do some fearless truth-telling. Now, he absolutely nailed the message, but the response was vicious, because it's a historical fact that not everyone wants to hear the message about Jesus – not because the message is boring and irrelevant, but because human beings like being in charge. Jesus will always be great news for the humble and a threat to the proud. This gang were the latter and Stephen's message threatened the very heart of their power, livelihood and reputation.

In Stephen's final moments, they began to throw their rocks at him. I find it incredible that he wasn't visibly overcome with panic or distress. This was not your usual stoning. Like the lady in the story, the record of his last moments shows him being caught up in the glow of a vision of heaven, his heart steady, his eyes fixed on Jesus standing in awesome glory, his heart rising in anticipation of finally meeting his Saviour. The onlookers must have seen this difference in Stephen's face to record it for us. They must have seen a radiant smile as he looked up, ready for the Lord to receive his spirit, at the very same time as his body was being smashed up by the rocks.

I think both the lady and this famous disciple had something in common. I think they had hope. Not the 'I hope things are going to be OK' kind, but a deep, Spirit-birthed certainty that death would not harm them, and that Jesus would carry them through it.

This kind of hope is the game-changer when it comes to dying. It completely rewrites the script. Our faithless world tells us we have everything to fear and everything to lose. But our hope in Christ reminds us we have absolutely nothing to fear and everything to look forward to. This hope was alive in them because they knew Jesus intimately and they walked by faith. These two facts meant that in the moment many of us dread, they soared. Instead of being captivated by the fear of death, they were captivated by His gaze. The worst-case scenario for most of us was the very best thing that happened to them.

Have you ever met anyone with hope like that?

I'd go as far as to say, I'm not sure they really *felt* death. In their preoccupation with Him, they were supernaturally delivered from the darkness of the experience. Jesus was faithful to His promise that He would never leave them.[2]

Now, were they just uniquely blessed? Could it be true that even we could go out with a smile? Well, I can't presume to know how we will leave *here* for *there*. We may or may not know about it. It may come quickly, or gradually. But I do believe this same hope is available to us in Christ. It is activated by our faith and grows stronger each day in a close friendship with Him, completely releasing us to approach our final moments with a fearless peace. We can know in a life-transforming way that our best-case scenario is always ahead of us because Jesus overcame death, removed its power over us and prepared a life on the other side superseding anything we could experience *here*.

It's time to change the script, because there is good news. And the good news is that in that moment, we will not *end*, we will *transcend*.

---

[2] Matthew 28.20

Take it further

- Reflect on the 'script' leading your thoughts and feelings about dying. What is it telling you?

- What would it take this week to bring your relationship with Jesus to a place of greater intimacy?

- Start a journal, if you don't already have one. Write down any relevant thoughts. They might even be in song/poetry form, or drawing.

Take it to Jesus

Jesus, I want to know You in such a way that it changes my script on dying. Like Stephen, I want to see You at Your most beautiful, when life is most dark and difficult. I want to be able to smile because I know You have gone ahead of me and removed the power of death. Let hope come alive in me at this very moment, and let fear be overcome in the presence of Your all-conquering peace. Help me to begin to see all that You have blessed me with in the future, so that it transforms my today.
Amen.

Right from the inception of their faith, their perspective on the future seriously and wonderfully changed.

2
The Missing Peace

For we have heard of your faith in Christ Jesus
and your love for all of God's people, which
come from your confident hope of what God has
reserved for you in heaven. You have had this
expectation ever since you first heard the truth
of the Good News.
Colossians 1:4-5

Every experienced puzzler knows it's a bad idea to buy puzzles at garage sales.

Why? Because, like me, you will spend hours putting the 5,000 pieces together only to find at the end at least one piece is missing, right? It's under somebody's dining room table or down the back of their sofa, laughing at me. It's anywhere but where it should be – in my puzzle box. Can you feel my frustration? Yep, I just bought a 4,999-piece puzzle destined to leave me seriously unsatisfied.

Now, the apostle Paul had spotted something about the expectation of the Colossian church and pinned it on one of the *first* pieces of the faith puzzle to fall into place. Did you catch it? A 'confident hope of what God has reserved for you in heaven'. Wow, right from the inception of their faith, their perspective on the future seriously and wonderfully changed. Not only had they received forgiveness, but the Colossian script on dying had been rewritten in an encounter with the Spirit of Jesus.

But my experience during twenty years of pastoral ministry has led me to the conclusion that this 'confident hope' is a missing puzzle piece for many Christians today. And this may explain our missing *peace*. Despite our having heard and responded to the gospel, the script on dying has remained largely untouched, and not many confidently know what the things reserved for us in heaven are. In fact, this may be a problem for the wider Church in our generation. You see, we have access to more knowledge than ever before, but I think there's a gap where our 'confident hope' should be.

Have we lost a piece of the faith puzzle?

Many people I have spoken to still view their future fearfully rather than hopefully. The expectation of the resurrection that emboldened the early Christians through suffering seems to have escaped the contemporary Church. We hold on to everything *here* so tightly, we struggle to give it away. And when death impacts families and churches, many are confused and angry with God for taking *here* away, as if He has failed them.

Many of the most-purchased Christian books and highest-attended Christian conferences major on healing. I believe in the healing power of the name of Jesus, but I also think it's possible that the queues of anxious Christians desperate to find the latest mechanism or a miracle to avoid dying is evidence of a hope gap. Instead of healing being a means of experiencing and advancing the kingdom of God on earth, it seems to me to be more about retaining the old life.

Perhaps the Church is too *now* biased. We emphasise the impact of the cross on the *now*. We love the *now* messages that inspire a more fruitful Christian lifestyle. We talk about justice on the earth *now*. We passionately want people to see and grasp what God is doing for them *now*. I know I have played my part in this, preaching for many hours on all the above. I have spent far fewer helping people to grab hold of an eternal perspective, or enabling them to see the hope of the resurrection, or describing to them our inheritance in heaven in all its comforting dimensions. And while all these messages are good, it just seems that the *now* ones get much more airtime. Speaking about *there* can feel like wasting time better spent on *here*.

I'm sure there could be many reasons for the hope gap, but however we got here, we need to go in search of that peace that will make a massive difference to our lives. We could join the lady, the stoned disciple, the apostle Paul and the Colossian church in a fearless view of the end of *here* if we find it.

What's certain is that, if we don't, the hole it leaves behind will catch us out just when we need it most, because being encouraged about the future is instrumental to good spiritual, mental and emotional health. It helped Jesus endure the cross. It helped Paul and others face persecution even to death. It helped previous generations of Christians cope with world wars, famines and disease, and it will help us in the twenty-first century handle anything that comes *our* way. Without it, we may find ourselves in 'the valley of the shadow of death' with no rod or staff to hold on to.[3]

I grew up in a Christian family and attended church. My picture of heaven was largely shaped by old hymns, none quite as memorable as this one (sing along if you know it):

> A robe of white, a crown of gold,
> A harp, a home, a mansion fair
> A victor's palm, a joy untold
> Are mine when I get there.[4]

Now, while certainly a catchy number, I have to say it didn't chime with me as something to look forward to. I wanted to know if football and barbecues and cars and chocolate were possible in the next life, but I was being offered a harp. It felt like my picture of heaven was built on things I didn't really want. My dear grandparents once bought me a cheese grater as a gift. Now, don't get me wrong, I like cheese as much as the next man, but that was not the gift I really wanted from a holiday trip to the Netherlands. I would have taken several things before a cheese grater, including, yep, nothing at all, before that made my list.

For me, heaven was like a big celestial cheese grater. I could get into the mansion idea, but all in all, this wasn't doing much for my view of heaven. *Here* seems better than

---

[3] Psalm 23:4, ESV.

[4] Taken from the hymn 'Marching on in the Light of God'. Author: Robert Johnson (1854–98). First published 1883, public domain.

there on a like-for-like comparison, if that old song is the criteria. It felt like a dream I couldn't get hold of and look forward to which, in turn, led to an avoidance of heaven and a deep wish to stay *here* if possible.

So when I went through a season of anxiety connected to health concerns, I realised I didn't have a good enough grip on the whole of the message Jesus brought. My long nights of fearfulness revealed that I was still operating on an old script, and that His gospel had not penetrated deep enough into my soul to really uphold me. I knew it provided a place for me in heaven and that I should not fear any outcome, but the reality was I *did* fear. I was missing the peace and 'confident hope' of the gospel. I was preoccupied with suffering and death in a way that overcame my faith, instead of being preoccupied with Jesus and experiencing the peace of faith in *Him*.

It was then that I began to explore the Bible for something deeper. I discovered a heaven that had been missing from my theology. I found an eternal perspective that dispelled much of my anxiety, and a presence that calmed my troubled sea of thoughts. I found the Jesus of my future, not only of my past, and in Him I found the piece of the puzzle I was missing.

So if you long for what the lady, the disciple and the Colossians had, I am here to tell you it is possible. If you think you've lost that piece of the puzzle and fear is overcoming your faith, let's go and look for it. And if your struggle to understand *there* isn't helping you *here*, then you've picked up the right book. I want to take you on a journey that I hope will help you experience more of the 'confident hope'.

When we place our faith in Jesus, we are born again[5] into an eternal state of life, so that we can leave these dying bodies with that lady's smile. The apostle Paul had it too, and it's to him that we need to turn next.

Take it further

- Reflect on the 'missing piece' analogy when it comes to your knowledge of heaven and the resulting confidence in your hope. What are you seeing?

- Think of a person who displays this 'confident hope'. How could you learn from or appreciate them more?

Take it to Jesus

Jesus, I want every heavenly blessing that belongs to me. I don't want to miss out on the hope You have won for me, and the way it will transform my life. Thank You for the cross, and for the resurrection. May both truths penetrate my heart, renew my mind and chase away the shadows of shame and fear from my soul. Strengthen my faith, teach me Your Word, draw close to me as I draw close to You in this issue and settle once and for all a brave confidence in me about life beyond the grave.
Amen.

---

[5] See John 3:1-21.

There will be no resentment in Paul's dying, because nothing on earth is worth more than Christ to him. He has let go of *here,* before *here* has let go of him.

3
Paul's Swansong

But I will rejoice even if I lose my life, pouring it
out like a liquid offering to God.
Philippians 2:17

I probably don't know enough about swans, but...

I've heard of the term 'swansong' usually referring to the way a person says farewell and finishes on a high. A retiring musician may call their final tour their 'swansong'.

Apparently, it's rooted in ancient cultures that believed that swans would sing beautifully just before they were about to die. This idea was written into poetry and philosophy, and over time became *a thing*. Swan experts (yes, they exist) say it's not true, but it's too late for their smug corrections. It's a thing and everyone knows it.

Now, Paul must have known something about swans because Philippians 2:17 must be the most countercultural, mind-bending text in the whole New Testament.

Paul has decided he will *rejoice* in the event he loses his life, like it's the one final opportunity to give something to God as an offering of worship. Most Christians I know would not view their dying as an opportunity to worship one last time. Most of us see worship as a song, but not as our swansong.

Do you know anyone who thinks about dying like this? I think Paul is on to something seriously good, and we need to catch up.

> For to me, to live is Christ and to die is gain.
> *Philippians 1:21 (NIV)*

Here's what I have come to term 'the two most common responses to death among Christians beginning with the letter R'. Catchy, I know. They are *resentment* and *resignation*.

Resentment occurs when we have placed our hope in the wrong things. This may just be a problem for the wealthier West, but we have made life about being as comfortable as we can. Many reading this book will have food and clothing, some will enjoy holidays and property, cars and Christmas presents. Perhaps you dine out occasionally and attend a good church when life is a season of blessing and you're not restricted by viral pandemics.

We like a lot about this life. Is any of that bad? The answer is no *and* yes. No, it's not bad because it's God's creative blessing in our lives. Yes, it is bad if it becomes more important than Jesus to us. The Bible calls this 'idolatry', which is when a 'good thing' becomes a 'god thing'.

Paul says that 'to live is Christ'. We could replace 'Christ' in that statement with all sorts of things: relationships, careers, kids, money, hobbies – you name it. But the problem is that when we do that we cannot say as Paul did next, 'to die is gain'. With a person, a dream or a possession as the first focus of our life, death is only ever going to be a catastrophic loss for us.

We will want to hold on to those things because they are life to us. We will want to avoid death because it threatens our self-made slice of heaven. Loss will cause us to be resentful towards God for taking whatever or whoever 'it' is away from us. Instead of being filled with the hope of *there*, we become angry or resentful at our spoiled heaven *here*.

Resignation occurs when we have battled long and hard in prayer, and on the occasions when no healing has been granted, death can feel more like a defeat than an offering or a victory. Not knowing why, and broken by grief, we can resign ourselves to a position that accepts God must have an answer, but that we will never grasp it and just have to accept our sad lot.

I understand our desire to keep someone with us for as long as possible. We don't want to lose loved ones, and so we pray passionately. But faith for healing entirely detached from faith in a resurrection to new life can have the effect of producing this disappointment. Unanswered prayers leave us focusing on what we *don't* know, rather than what we *do* know.

Resignation, on the face of it, can look a little like faith, but it's a negative place to live. We are fighting to trust in a God who apparently didn't come through for us, instead of celebrating that He has in a better way than we could have asked or imagined.[6]

The problem with Christian resignation in the face of death is that it's not a great witness to others. People are drawn to faith when we suffer loss and still sing of God's amazing goodness. It begs the most important of questions – how, and why? Resignation only confirms the world's fears and is met with a knowing pat on the shoulder. Hope and faith in these crucial moments floor people because they don't see them everywhere. Miracles always stand out.

Read Paul's approach to his own death again. Can you see any hint of the two Rs in his words? I think not. He calls it 'gain', which is the exact opposite of 'loss'. There will be no resentment in Paul's dying, because nothing on earth is worth more than Christ to him. He has let go of *here,* before *here* has let go of him.

In Philippians 2:18, he tells us that he will 'rejoice'. Rejoicing leaves no room for resentment and keeps us from the pitfall of resignation. Rejoicing keeps us in the spiritual state of faith. To the person who rejoices in every circumstance,[7] life is an anthem of worship building towards a crescendo where the greatest moment is the final note – the swansong! Paul is determined he is not going out in a key of despair and defeat. He has cultivated a life of rejoicing, and he is building up to the final and best offering – his body.

Only on the solid foundation of 'confident hope' could Paul, and any of us, face death with such a countercultural

[6] See Ephesians 3:20, NIV.
[7] See 1 Thessalonians 5:16-18, NIV.

perspective. His mind had been renewed.[8] Paul didn't just preach the good news, he also believed it right down to his core, and this hope produced a new script that changed everything for him.

If 'gain' and 'rejoice' are not somewhere in our vocabulary when it comes to our dying, then one reason may be that we are gripping something here too tightly. We may have made a good thing into a god thing. What could that be?

> I'm torn between two desires: I long to go and be with Christ, which would be far better for me. But for your sakes, it is better that I continue to live.
> *Philippians 1:23-24*

We all experience loss in life.

I lost my hair way too early. I remember walking out of the barber's at the age of twenty, looking at my reflection in the glass window of the bus stop and seeing far too much of my scalp. I thought the barber had been a bit too friendly with his tools, but little did I know that this day would be the beginning. It wasn't so much of a receding hairline as it was a full retreat.

What makes my sense of loss worse is the fact that I'm frequently required to clean the plugholes in my house because my wife's locks keep blocking them. It's like the hair is taunting me.

Whether it's losing our hair, our health, a job, a precious belonging or a loved one, loss impacts us all, and it can be

---

[8] See Romans 12:2, NIV.

very painful at times. And sudden changes can have an enormous impact on our mental health, as we learned through the Covid pandemic.

We could confuse Paul's statements about rejoicing in his dying with the notion that he had nothing valuable to leave behind. Perhaps he was a loner, or insensitive, or unfeeling. But Paul wasn't detached from others at all. He had many deep and profound friendships that would have created a sense of loss between Paul and them. He explained to the Philippians that he was 'torn' by his desire to stay *here* and go *there*, and I think this is a healthy tension.

Like us, of course, Paul would experience sadness and the grief of separation from loved ones. Rejoicing is not the absence of sadness, but rather the choice to put that sadness into the context of hopefulness; to see it in the light of eternity, rather than the moment alone. Paul was able to rejoice his way through the sadness of leaving people he loved, knowing he would ultimately be reunited with them.

For those whose eternal destinies were still unknown, Paul was able to rejoice in the knowledge that God was more than able to continue the unfinished business of the kingdom without him.

As a pastor, I, too, have lost and buried friends and family. These moments are always painful, but I thank God I have somewhere to put that pain. Like Paul, I have found a hope perspective that keeps resentment and resignation from warping or stealing my faith. I can simultaneously mourn the loss and rejoice in the hope I have. And I hope to approach my own death as Paul did, ready to offer my body, the last thing I have to give to God in a final act of worship.

But to really hope amid loss, and to think of dying as gain, we must have some idea of what we are preparing ourselves for. Let's go on a journey and imagine *there* with a little help from the Bible.

Take it further

- Read the book of Philippians with a focus on the author, Paul. What are you catching in Paul's outlook on life that inspires you? What instructions does he give to us so that we can experience the same outlook?

- If appropriate, consider who you have in your world to help you process feelings of sadness and loss, or connect with a grief counsellor. Or, if helpful, see the list at the end of the book of helpful websites offering support.

Take it to Jesus

Jesus, I want my whole life to be an offering of worship, and my last notes to be my swansong. Help me to live with a stronger hold on You. The enemy wants to use earthly loss to steal my faith and make me turn on You, but You are proving my faith in every trial so that it stands forever. Help me not to waver in resentment or resignation but to rejoice in the truth that You have

overcome the world and the grave, enabling me to live
with holy optimism in every season.
Amen.

I'm convinced that one of the reasons we struggle to benefit from the hope of living after dying is that we haven't really grasped the knowledge that what we're holding on to so very tightly *here* is a very poor version of *there*.

4
Imagining Paradise

I desire to depart and be with Christ, which is
better by far.
Philippians 1:23 (NIV)

And Jesus replied, 'I assure you, today you will
be with me in paradise.'
Luke 23:43

I once stayed in a hotel where the roof was falling in.

On a church mission trip to the beautiful nation of
Zimbabwe, my team and I arrived in the capital city,
Harare. We were taken to a large and grand-looking hotel
built when Zimbabwe was Rhodesia and under British
rule. The stately architecture reminiscent of central
London hinted at this colonial past. The majestic entrance
hall must have once entertained very important people.
Few could have imagined then that this building would
struggle to achieve one star and that I would be able to
afford to stay in it.

First, it was dark inside in a way that made you think it was closed for business. This was probably a management tactic to get you to miss the large chunks of the ceiling in the entrance hall that had fallen in, and the mortar and lath that were visible. A decorator had not touched a single room since probably the early twentieth century. There were loose electrical sockets in our bathroom, of all places, with wires exposed, and I had never felt scared in a lift before, until that day. You'd have a job finding a hotel in worse repair.

Under new ownership, it still stood, but any glory had left the building.

Now, our planet is not what it used to be, either. It's not creation's fault; we subjected it to a slow decline the moment we told the Creator to step back and let us go it alone. This story is found in Genesis 3, where Adam and Eve chose to eat the fruit of the tree of the knowledge of good and evil in direct violation of God's command to leave it alone. The name of the tree should have given them a clue about the result. What this story about our earliest ancestors, trees, fruit, snakes and fig leaves is pointing to is a shift in ownership and the introduction of evil into the good creation. Our ancestors decided to go their own way. Like a gentleman, God respected our freedom to choose, and then we made the proverbial bed we're lying in. *Here* still has the remnants of all the good God designed it with, but it's no secret it's falling apart. It still stands, but we'd pay all the money in the world to remove its suffering, heal its environment, feed its children and cure its diseases if that would make the difference. Unfortunately, its repair is beyond the scope of all the money, governments and environmentalists in the world combined.

You see, under our ownership, it still stands, but the glory left the building when we told Him to.

So *there*, according to Paul, is far better than *here*. So much better, in fact, a resident *there* might think it strange we would want to hang on to *here* for so long. And yet we do. There is still a lot of good *here*, but I'm convinced that one of the reasons we struggle to benefit from the hope of living after dying is that we haven't really grasped the knowledge that what we're holding on to so very tightly *here* is a very poor version of *there*. We've become accustomed to the décor of our current hotel, and we cannot imagine that somewhere five-star even exists.

I loved my first car. It was a red, 1980 Mark 1 Vauxhall Astra. It had probably been owned by twelve other boy racers before it reached my hands, but as a seventeen-year-old desperate for freedom, I couldn't envisage being any happier than I was with that car. I had finally made it. Then I crashed it. Literally three days before I passed my driving test my foot slipped off the brake pedal (it was wet!), hit the accelerator and flew me into the back of the very disgruntled driver in front. I painted 'ouch' across the dented bonnet and continued to drive that car for a whole year. The next car wasn't much better, but every scrappy car I bought gave me the same feeling – paradise.

That Vauxhall Astra certainly wasn't a Mercedes; I had to pull a manual choke, wind the windows up and down and find natural means to warm my driver's seat, but boy, did I think I'd made it!

To press home the analogy, we're living in this 'old model'. We're very attached to it because it's all we have right now. But what if I told you that God was preparing something far better? What if the glory could return? What would *that* earth look like? If we could know what eternity promises us, then maybe we'd be more excited for it, and less likely to be seduced by the present world.

I once heard a story about a man who made a deal with God to bring one suitcase with him to heaven. He wanted more, but God had relented on His 'no belongings allowed' rule and let the guy take the one. The time came for him to leave the earth, and sure enough, he arrived at the gates of heaven, where St Peter waited to greet him.

'No suitcases allowed,' Peter rightly declared, but after further conversation and a check on the heavenly intranet, Peter discovered this man indeed had a pass.

'I'll have to check your case before you enter,' Peter said, and with that he opened the zip to discover that the man had filled the case with bars of pure gold, purchased by selling all his earthly possessions.

Puzzled and bemused, Peter turned to the man and asked, 'Why did you bring pavement?'[9]

If the best we can attain *here* just about makes the pavement *there*, then what must *there* be like? Will it resemble life *here* in any way? Paul tells us:

> No eye has seen, no ear has heard,
> and no mind has imagined

---

[9] Original author unknown. My paraphrase. Source: leiningers.com/heaven.html (accessed 30th December 2020). See Revelation 21:21.

what God has prepared
for those who love him.
1 Corinthians 2:9

No mind has imagined…

It's difficult to imagine the unlimited lengths of exploration, innovation, creativity and fun that could be achieved in partnership with an all-powerful Friend with every resource at His disposal, and forever to do it in. Our brains are simply too small to take it all in. I guess God created a large universe for a reason, and the life we currently experience is a teeny, tiny fraction of what is possible with God.

This verse puts our future life in the category of 'too good', not less good.

Paul also tells the Corinthians in his second letter about an experience he had had, that must have shaped him considerably:

> I was caught up to the third heaven fourteen years ago. Whether I was in my body or out of my body, I don't know – only God knows. Yes, only God knows whether I was in my body or outside my body. But I do know that I was caught up to paradise and heard things so astounding that they cannot be expressed in words, things no human is allowed to tell.
> *2 Corinthians 12:2-4*

From that moment he lost any notion that he would find something *here* more fulfilling than *there*. Totally astounded by what he saw, he just wanted to take as many people *there* with him as he possibly could. I think he was able to say, 'I desire to depart and be with Christ, which is better by far,'[10] because he had caught a glimpse of life in His presence, and he described this 'third heaven' as being 'paradise'.

Paradise is exactly how Jesus described it to the thief on the cross.[11] While we are entering a subject of great mystery, scholars suggest this paradise refers to our being consciously present with Jesus Christ where He is immediately following our death, while we await resurrection to our new bodies on a new earth, where He will then live with us.[12] Paradise is described in theological language as an 'intermediate state' of existence. Its meaning suggests a beautiful retreat for us to await the resurrection. It's where the lady who died in church, Stephen the martyr and all who die believing in Jesus are right now. And if the waiting room is a paradise – then what's coming next on the new earth He creates will be nothing less.

So will life on the new paradise earth resemble *here* in anyway?

I'm not sure where your mind goes when you think of 'paradise', but I'm reminded of the rare occasions I've been blessed enough to experience a touch of it: sipping strawberry smoothies on sun-drenched Greek islands where hills covered in olive trees roll down to meet the warm, turquoise ocean; the savannah of Africa, where

---

[10] Philippians 1:23, NIV.

[11] See Luke 23:43.

[12] N T Wright, *Surprised by Hope* (San Francisco, CA: HarperOne, 2007), p41.

majestic animals roam under incredible sunsets; or the simply breath-taking mountain scapes of the Austrian Alps made famous by *The Sound of Music*.

Can you imagine it? Glorious.

Perhaps you dream of the paradise of being debt-free, or physically healed in some way, or employed in a job you believe in. Maybe it's retirement with the time and health to enjoy it, or a romantic relationship, or the excitement of a newborn baby arriving in the family, or buying the house of your dreams. Whether present realities or a hope of yours for the future, these are amazing experiences also.

Maybe it's in an accomplishment of an extraordinary feat, or seeing your team win the final of the tournament, or enjoying a piece of art or music that pulls on all your heart strings.

These can all be truly memorable moments and you may be on cloud nine, but your cloud doesn't even get close to what I think Jesus and Paul are describing.

Remember, Jesus and His new friend, the penitent thief, were leaving all these good things behind *for* paradise.

I love to watch trailers of movies coming soon. The trailer tells me what I'm going to enjoy about the movie, but I don't stop at the trailer. I think about life *here* this way: every good thing you and I experience is just a trailer of the whole movie *there*. Far from God undoing the good we have experienced *here*, these things will continue perfectly, in a far richer experience of them. It's going to be stunning, awe-inspiring, breath-taking and exhilarating.

That love you experience *here* will be heightened and fulfilled *there*. That place you go to *here* with the view that makes your mouth hit the floor in awe is going to be everywhere, *there*. The warmth of a group of friends, the taste of your favourite food, the euphoria of a great worship experience, the satisfaction of doing something meaningful – all these *goods* are pointing to something greater and lasting *there*.

The wonders I've described are only really shadows of paradise, rather than paradise itself. Yes, we are going to get *there* and realise what *here* was trying to tell us all along.

Paradise suggests to us that a more beautiful existence than this one awaits us. The Bible ignites our imagination when it tells us that there will be a recreation of the heavens and the earth, everything made new, and everything made to last:

> Then I saw a new heaven and a new earth, for the old heaven and the old earth had disappeared.
> *Revelation 21:1*

And in our resurrected bodies there will be no more division between us and Jesus. We will live as one with Him. Our relationship with Him will enhance our relationships with others, not replace them, and better than every created thing we will experience and enjoy for eternity will be our experience of His intimate presence and every awesome attribute of His nature freely shared with us. His glory will inspire our deepest awe, greatest affection and highest praise – an eternity of worship songs reflecting His goodness.

> Look, God's home is now among his people! He
> will live with them, and they will be his people.
> God himself will be with them.
> *Revelation 21:3*

When Jesus comes to take us to paradise, at whatever age, make no mistake – He has done us a momentous good. He has not failed us. Our seasons of trial are over, our metamorphosis is complete; no dents, no scratches; we will exchange this old model for the life we were made for. And we will see Him face to face. His beauty and glory and presence will be so fantastically thrilling to our hearts that we will say with Paul that being *with* Christ is 'better by far'![13]

Because everything will be as it should be, it will not occur to us to look back longingly at this life, in just the same way I do not look back at my Vauxhall Astra with a busted front end wishing I still owned it. The Hebrew language has a word for this new reality – *'Shalom'*. It means peace, and it's to the subject of peace we turn next.

Take it further

• Reflecting on the mistake of the man in the story who took a suitcase of gold to heaven, what do you think *will* last?

---

[13] Philippians 1:23, NIV.

- Take some time out with the Holy Spirit. You could go for a walk in a place of natural beauty, or a park, or your garden. If this isn't possible for you, if you can, look out at the sky. Take a moment to worship Him as you consider the work of His fingers[14] and thank Him for His promise of a new earth.

Take it to Jesus

Jesus, I want to live life looking forward to paradise! I want my thinking to be shaped by the hope and anticipation of something better to come, rather than nostalgia or dread. Chase away the shadows of fear and despair from my soul. Ignite my imagination with a heavenly vision. Fill my mind and heart with all that will be when I join You in paradise and the life to come.
Amen.

---

[14] See Psalm 8:3.

What's true for nature will be true for every one of us – no more dog-eat-dog living, no strife, no natural disasters, no corruption in politics, no international spies, no national borders or racial divisions; the end of wars, the removal of weapons, the uniting of people around one holy presence, a paradise of 'peace on earth'.

5
Leading Lions

Of the greatness of his government and peace
there will be no end.
Isaiah 9:7 (NIV)

It turns out predicting the future is fraught with difficulty.

In the year 1800, Dionysius Lardner, professor of natural philosophy and astronomy from University College London, predicted that people would not survive train journeys because of their high speed's effect on our ability to breathe.

In 1902, Simon Newcomb, a mathematician and astronomer, predicted that flying machines would never take off. He believed that they were too heavy and there would be little usefulness in trying.

In 1977, Ken Olsen, president, chair and founder of Digital Equipment Corporation, could not see any reason that a person would need their own computer.[15]

I'm pretty hit and miss when it comes to predicting the future also.

I predicted I'd be married with kids in my twenties. I predicted I'd get a degree. I predicted my favourite football team would win the championship every year for several years. Wrong on all counts.

Yes, the future is a tricky customer to pin down. But if I *could* know what the future holds, I'd be a billionaire. I mean, just imagine being able to know the next batch of lottery numbers before they're pulled from the bowl, or the results of the next great sporting event. That kind of knowledge would really transform my life right now.

Here's a great truth – we *do* know the future, and it *can* transform our now. Our 'confident hope' is made confident by the fact that the Bible is astoundingly accurate at the business of future telling. We can fully trust it.

Take the prophet Isaiah, for example. Isaiah lived seven centuries before Jesus and was called by God to speak to the nation of Israel on His behalf. Some of the words God gave Isaiah to share spoke of future events. He is most famous perhaps for the prophecies he recorded about the Messiah – the saviour who would come and release the people from suffering and sin. He said the following:

---

[15] Source: www.boredpanda.com/bad-future-predictions-timeline-history/?utm_source=google&utm_medium=organic&utm_campaign=organic (accessed 24th May 2021).

The Messiah would be born of a virgin (Isaiah 7:14).

A messenger would prepare the way for Him (Isaiah 40:3-5).

He would have a ministry of miracles (Isaiah 35:5-6).

He would teach in parables (Isaiah 6:8-10).

He would be rejected by His people (Isaiah 53:3).

He would be silent before His accusers (Isaiah 53:7).

He would be crucified with criminals (Isaiah 53:12).

He would be buried with the rich (Isaiah 53:9).

He would be resurrected, and make people right with God (Isaiah 53.11)

The Gospel of Matthew goes to great lengths to show how these predictions came true in the life of the man we know as Jesus. Isaiah's writings were well known and established as Hebrew scripture long before Jesus lived. We can only marvel, then, at the accuracy of his words concerning things that actually happened long after his death.

So when Isaiah makes predictions beyond even our age, he has my full attention. The following prophecy may relate to life during the millennial reign of Christ on earth – a period foretold in the book of Revelation. Or it could be speaking of life on the new earth following the resurrection. It's also possible his prophecy reflects some truth in both future realities. Either way, this passage seems to describe in some detail the vision of life under the government of Christ, and His endless peace. Look at what he says:

> The wolf will live with the lamb,
> the leopard will lie down with the goat,
> the calf and the lion and the yearling together;
> and a little child will lead them.
> The cow will feed with the bear,
> their young will lie down together,
> and the lion will eat straw like the ox.
> The infant will play near the cobra's den,
> and the young child will put its hand into the viper's nest.
> They will neither harm nor destroy
> on all my holy mountain,
> for the earth will be filled with the knowledge of the LORD
> as the waters cover the sea.
> *Isaiah 11:6-9 (NIV)*

God, speaking through Isaiah, describes His vision of the future using nature to explain the difference between *here* and *there* under the eternal government of Jesus. And God sees children leading lions.

This is astonishing if you've ever met or heard a lion in the wild.

Here, lions are the unrivalled king of the animal kingdom. Their roar is unmistakable and frightening, their claws sharp as knives and their strength legendary. Lions represent power, dominance and ferocious violence. Humans may have captured them, but they will not willingly be friendly pets.

There is described, then, as a complete role reversal. It's upside down. The smallest among us will be able to lead the lion. The humble will have dominance over the once proud. The 'last will be first'.[16] Peace will replace power. We can take from this vision that life will not resemble the order of things *here* in the slightest.

Under His 'government and peace',[17] which will know no end, all creation will live in harmony, resulting in true safety and security. The lamb won't need a fence or a big burly shepherd with a rod to keep it safe from the wolf. You and I won't need our walls and fences and well-trained inner defence mechanisms to keep us from being hurt. The goat can sleep easy alongside its stalker, the leopard. No one will be after you or against you. Why? Because there will no longer be an enemy, hunter, menace or violence, anywhere, any more.

Breathe that in for a moment.

Imagine never having to brace for impact.

Isaiah describes the likely end of the carnivorous age. Lions will eat straw and be satisfied with it. Food will be sourced without the need for harm or destruction. Meat eaters among us may wonder how on earth we could survive without steak and bacon – and I know this will

---

[16] Matthew 19:30, NIV.
[17] Isaiah 9:7, NIV.

require great faith from some – but I'm sure all the food God prepares in paradise will taste so fresh and good to us we will not miss it in the slightest.

Can you taste it?

Isaiah describes a world where children will flourish and will not experience pain. Children will lead lions and they will place their hands into a viper den without fear because snakes won't have a deadly bite. Eden will be restored for them.

This is not just God painting a picture of paradise. It's what you and I would want for our kids, if we have them. It's the dream of a good Father.

What's true for nature will be true for every one of us – no more dog-eat-dog living, no strife, no natural disasters, no corruption in politics, no international spies, no national borders or racial divisions; the end of wars, the removal of weapons, the uniting of people around one holy presence, a paradise of 'peace on earth'.[18]

Isaiah's prophecy in chapter 9 of his book, noted at the beginning of this chapter, sums up our hope, then, in a beautiful way: 'Of the greatness of his government and peace there will be no end.'[19] His rule will establish unending peace on earth. It's hard to imagine right now that these things could take place when we live in a world and culture so full of the lions of power and politics, greed and violence. It's our culture to think it's normal and meant to be this way. Lions are supposed to dominate the weak, right? We can hardly imagine what any other world would look like.

---

[18] Luke 2:14
[19] Isaiah 9:7, NIV.

But to see what eternity is like we will need to learn to see through the eyes of a Father preparing a place for His children to thrive. No wonder Jesus said that we would need to become like children[20] to enter it.

Readers of the Old Testament were quite aware of Isaiah's prophecy of a peace that would know 'no end'.[21] What they didn't know was when these things would take place, or how.

> As they strained to see him rising into heaven, two white-robed men suddenly stood among them. 'Men of Galilee,' they said, 'why are you standing here staring into heaven? Jesus has been taken from you into heaven, but someday he will return from heaven in the same way you saw him go!'
> *Acts 1:10-11*

'Someday'. This is the nature of biblical future prediction. It describes the *state* of the future, but it does not give us the *date* of the future. It provides us with imagery that helps us to perceive the times and seasons we are in, and it gives us great promises to strengthen our hope.

This branch of theology is known as eschatology and is concerned with all the events leading up to the coming new earth. It attempts (with a variety of results) to build a picture of the future from various passages of Scripture yet to be fulfilled. It is often avoided by Christians in favour of simpler, and more immediately relevant,

---

[20] See Matthew 18:3.
[21] Isaiah 9:7, NIV.

subjects. Not many people want to read about the apocalypse over breakfast!

While this is understandable, these apocalyptic passages were not given to frighten the followers of Jesus, but to encourage our hope. You see, no matter how difficult things become *here*, no matter how deep our suffering, or how dominant the lions of our age, we know that Jesus will return. Not all of us will die, but those who are living when He returns will be 'caught up' with Him and transformed into new bodies, according to 1 Corinthians 15:51-53 and 1 Thessalonians 4:17. And we know that we will appear before Christ and be ushered to a new earth for us to spend eternity upon.[22]

While the world fears what *could* happen, we know what *will* happen. We know because Jesus has already gone ahead of us and revealed it to us so that our hearts will not succumb to panic when seasons change, but rather rise in faith and expectation of the coming kingdom of peace.

Take it further

• When God describes the future through Isaiah, He reveals not only His Lordship but also His Fatherhood, by emphasising in detail the safety that little children will experience there. What does this tell you?

---

[22] See 2 Corinthians 5:10; Revelation 21:1.

- Take a moment to pray and reflect on an area of your life that you could bring the peace and reconciliation of Jesus into.

Take it to Jesus

Jesus, before You come to govern the world with peace, govern me. Remove any way in me that does not produce peace. I want my life to be filled with Your knowledge, so order my life according to Your kingdom truths. Help me to be a peace-receiver and a peacemaker so that more and more I reflect the life that is to come – the one You are preparing for me and all Your children.

Amen.

There will be no countdown, no endings, no looking back as if the best days are behind us.

6
Unlimited Time

Now we live with great expectation, and we
have a priceless inheritance – an inheritance that
is kept in heaven for you, pure and undefiled,
beyond the reach of change and decay.
1 Peter 1:3-4

I was in one of the most secure places on planet Earth.

The Yeoman of the Guard gave the command to cease
and desist taking photos in the Jewel House. I dare say few
rooms on the planet contain the kind of wealth that resides
in this vault of the Tower of London. It's a special place,
keeping artefacts from hundreds of years of British royal
history including imperial crowns, thousands of precious
jewels, sceptres, swords, golden tableware, priceless
artwork and clothes worn by kings and queens.

Apparently, some items in this precious hoard of
wealth, kept within a bomb-proof vault, surrounded by
security cameras and an army unit, could degrade under
the power of the humble camera flash.

But I know of a place even more secure, where something even more valuable is kept than all the crown jewels, awaiting *our* arrival. Peter is talking about our inheritance 'kept in heaven' where nothing can touch it or degrade it.

He describes it as 'priceless', which means that all the money in the world wouldn't touch its worth. This famous Jewel House, Fort Knox and the Bank of England will all fade in comparison to the wealth you and I will receive from Jesus when we get *there*.

So when we are resurrected to the new earth paradise God has promised us, what will we receive? We know we cannot imagine the fullness of what God has prepared,[23] but let's think about what we do know, and examine its value.

> Our earthly bodies are planted in the ground when we die, but they will be raised to live forever. Our bodies are buried in brokenness, but they will be raised in glory. They are buried in weakness, but they will be raised in strength. They are buried as natural human bodies, but they will be raised as spiritual bodies.
> *1 Corinthians 15:42-44*

Paul is addressing questions from the Corinthian church about the resurrection of our bodies on the new earth, and he responds with four descriptions of a transformation that will take place between *here* and *there*, each meeting a

---

[23] See 1 Corinthians 2:9.

profound desire within all of us. Beginning in this chapter, we will take each one in turn.

1. Planted in the ground … raised to live forever.

2. Buried in brokenness … raised in glory.

3. Buried in weakness … raised in strength.

4. Buried as natural human bodies … raised as spiritual bodies.

The first 'priceless inheritance' of the resurrection is *unlimited time*.

It was 28th August and I was mildly depressed. You may know the feeling. My holiday had come to an end, I was on the plane and I'd hit a massive wall of grey cloud that signalled my arrival at the coast of England. I was regretting the decision to stay in my holiday shorts and T-shirt as I made my way down the steps of the plane in what felt like arctic temperatures. My phone signal returned and a '467 unread emails' notification was the first thing I saw, followed by a reminder that the meetings would start again the next morning.

Now, I'm not against working. I like my work. I'm privileged to serve Jesus as a pastor, following my calling and helping people in need. It's just that I like sitting on a beach *more*. I'm joking, of course (I like the pool as well!).

It's endings that I struggle with; how about you? When something great is happening, I have an inbuilt desire for it to continue. I'm sure I'm not the only one. And when it comes to living, most people do not *want* it to end.

Countless billions of pounds are spent trying to discover cures and methods for extending life by just a few more years. Some people will move across the world;

others will invest in plastic surgery and many will adopt rigorous exercise routines and diets to get the edge. Time is probably the most valuable commodity in the world. We've managed to increase our average life expectancy in the West from the mid-fifties to the eighties in the last 100 years, but recently this has plateaued.[24] Our best efforts are having an almost negligible effect.

The world is obsessed with avoiding the end of our experience of life. We want more time. Ecclesiastes 3:11 explains why: 'He has planted eternity in the human heart.'

The reason we don't want to die is that we're not supposed to. This verse tells us that forever is in our DNA! Death is not natural; it's rather like an unwanted thief cutting in on the life God made and stealing from us what was always meant to be permanent. We were designed by God to keep on living and loving, which is why we are so angered and broken by death. It goes against our wiring.

But the inheritance being kept for us is unlimited time. There will be no countdown, no endings, no looking back as if the best days are behind us. Like God, we will exist *timelessly*. That doesn't mean there won't be 'time' necessarily, because it's a good way of ordering things; it's just that we won't be slaves to its gradually diminishing tick-tock, tick-tock…

We will not be consumed by the need to stay young or to fight the effects of ageing. We will not decry the return from a beautiful holiday, because there will always be another one, and another one, and another one…

---

[24] Source: www.kingsfund.org.uk/publications/whats-happening-life-expectancy-england (accessed 26th May 2021).

Life and love will go on, just as it should.

One objection to this idea of unlimited time is that it's the shortness and unpredictability of life here that brings immanent meaning and joy to our lives. If we had all the time in the universe, we would succumb to extreme boredom, essentially.

But if God can exist timelessly without monotony or emptiness, then it's reasonable to assume we will also. He will fill the unlimited time with everything we need for an abundant, purposeful life. Along with purpose, we will exist in relationship with one another in a universal family. We will not run out of parties, or of things to discover and do with one another.

Our 'priceless inheritance' *there* is the end of death, and this has always been God's plan since the very first moment we sinned and succumbed to its power over us.

> Then, when our dying bodies have been
> transformed into bodies that will never die,
> this Scripture will be fulfilled:
> 'Death is swallowed up in victory.
> O death, where is your victory?
> O death, where is your sting?'
> *1 Corinthians 15:54-55*

Like the spirit of this scripture, we will gloat in our victory over death. The great enemy will have been overcome once and for all. We will no longer feel its sting. What jewel on earth could compare with such a prize? Our profound desire for more time will be satisfied.

In fact, we will finally have time for everything.

Take it further

- 1 Peter 1:3 says, 'Now we live with great expectation ...' Reflect on the capacity of your own expectation. What would help you to make it greater?

- Paul tells us that our bodies will be '*planted* in the ground',[25] rather than *buried*. Consider the depth of meaning in this choice of metaphor, and journal your thoughts.

Take it to Jesus

Jesus, take my expectation level from small to great! Help me to see with ever-increasing excitement and confidence that I will be raised to live forever. Yes, I am counting down the days to my beginning rather than my end. Grace me with the ability to live with a smile where others despair, so that they may see the hope in me and ask about You.
Amen.

---

[25] 1 Corinthians 15:42, emphasis mine.

All our lost battles, miserable failures and silly mistakes will go down into the ground and we will rise overwhelmingly victorious, never to experience a single defeat again.

7
Unbelievable Glory

Our bodies are buried in brokenness, but they
will be raised in glory.
1 Corinthians 15:43

The second 'priceless inheritance' of the resurrection is an unbelievable *glory*.

Have you ever thought about your body in a negative light? I know I have and I'm sure just about everyone does at some point. We will not always be happy with ourselves and can find plenty of reasons to cover up. We all have bodily features we put up with and can list things we'd love to change but can't. We are like 'fragile clay jars', according to 2 Corinthians 4:7, which carries with it a sense of weakness, mediocrity or commonness, and certainly not the glorious. This missing 'glory' is why the world is full of people seeking change. It's why we yearn to be young, or different somehow. Driving this behaviour is a profound desire to be happy with ourselves. No one likes to think of themselves as clay; we want to be gold.

Every year, athletes compete with each other for the glory of having the title the 'World's Strongest Man'.[26] They compete by pulling trucks, lifting enormous weights and testing every muscle and fibre in their body to the extreme. If you've ever seen the event on TV, I'm sure, like me, you cannot help but be amazed by what a human body jacked up to its fullest capacity can achieve. Bristling with muscle, these are human bodies at their most gloriously powerful.

Famously – and perhaps controversially – some women compete to be recognised as the most beautiful woman in the world. With natural physical and facial features complemented by the latest fashion, expert make-up and a well-crafted speech, these women strive to exhibit the glory of beauty.

Or perhaps you've seen the competition for the best beard in the world? Yes, it happens. The World Beard and Moustache Championships® bring together some of the most eccentric and creative men to show off the glory of their well-kept and moulded facial hair.[27] It's impressive, to say the least!

These are just a few examples of humankind's attempts to reach this state of 'glory' we all desire. And they can work for a while. We can experience periods of self-happiness. The truth is, though, that no matter what the glory we create here with our current bodies – whether through training, enhancing, moulding, dressing or entirely transforming – the fact remains that it doesn't last long. The human body is, sadly, mortal. Whatever we

---

[26] theworldsstrongestman.com (accessed 26th May 2021).
[27] worldbeardchampionships.com (accessed 26th May 2021).

create of ourselves is subject to the frustration of being extremely temporary. We're all working with broken materials.

The body does not usually die with glory, either. Whether by age or by illness, suffering the loss of even basic functions can be difficult to endure and even harder to watch in the lives of those we love. Thank God we are blessed to live in an age of medicine that can remove much of the pain from the experience.

When Paul says that we are sown into the ground in 'brokenness', or 'dishonour' as the NIV translates, he is describing this gradual succumbing of the body to final defeat and humiliation. Even the strongest among us in their independence, physique, intelligence and ability are lost to a baby-like dependence on others again. Even the prettiest among us will wrinkle. You and I will suffer some considerable loss in the journey, if we make it that far.

I remember my last visit to the hospital before my grandmother's passing. It had only been a few days since I had last seen her and yet her appearance had completely changed. Her eyes were barely able to open, her skin a grey, lifeless colour and her breathing laboured. At first, I thought it was a different person in the room. There was little glory left in this 'fragile clay jar'.

Those who work in the profession of nursing see this side of life all the time. I am amazed at the dignity and kindness they continually give, bringing comfort to the dying. I imagine helping people through this process can be a difficult job.

But the promise is, 'Our bodies are buried in brokenness, but they will be raised in glory.' This means that everything about our body and being will glorify its Creator, forever, and our profound desire to be happy with ourselves will be finally met. We won't be embarrassed by imperfections, or experience bodily brokenness. We won't want to change a thing. Rather, our bodies will look and feel perfect, just as they should. Low self-esteem is not going to be a problem for us *there*.

The dignity we lose in dying will be restored. Defeat completely turned into victory. More than that, everything done in the body that kept us hiding in shame and dishonour *here* will be gone. The old hymn I mentioned earlier begins to make sense as a collection of metaphors:

> A robe of white, a crown of gold,
> A harp, a home, a mansion fair
> A victor's palm, a joy untold
> Are mine when I get there.

This chorus is about the unbelievably glorious state we will experience *there* in new bodies, each metaphor a 'priceless inheritance' awaiting us.

The 'robe of white'[28] is a biblical metaphor for a new glorious purity. The sin that once marred our glory and stained our honour is replaced with the brilliant, clean glory of a new, sinless-to-the-core nature. Peter states that we will 'participate in the divine nature' – which means we will share God's perfect attributes again, as we did at the beginning.[29] Our sin-soiled clothes will go down into

---

[28] See Revelation 6:11.

[29] 2 Peter 1:4, NIV.

the ground and we will rise *pure*. We will be truly beautiful from the inside out.

The 'crown of Gold' and the 'victor's palm' are biblical metaphors for a glorious victory and the peace that results.[30] We will have triumphed over every satanic strategy to rob us of eternal life. This will be known as the greatest victory in the universe. All earthly accomplishments will fade in comparison to this one. All our lost battles, miserable failures and silly mistakes will go down into the ground and we will rise overwhelmingly victorious, never to experience a single defeat again.

A 'harp' is a metaphor of a new, glorious state.[31] Did you know the harp in its day was the most eye-catching, elegant, beautiful instrument, played among the elites of society? The idea here is that our position is raised to that of the elite, royal classes. We are among the highly honoured. We will enjoy the finest feasts, no expense spared, and our sound – yes, we will be able to sing in tune. Our spiritual poverty will go down into the ground and we rise *significantly rich*.

The 'home' and a 'mansion fair' are no doubt inspired by John 14:1-3. Jesus tells the disciples that He must go and prepare a home with 'many rooms' for us,[32] so that we can always be where He is. So these descriptions speak of a delightful resting place in that eternal home.

We will be finally and completely satisfied, prosperous, honoured and rewarded and at home with Christ – our greatest prize. We will look around at our new life and be

---

[30] See Psalm 21:3; John 12:13; Revelation 7:9.

[31] See Revelation 15:2.

[32] NIV.

ecstatic. Our humiliation will go down into the ground and we will rise in a bodily state of glory, never to be unhappy with ourselves again.

Can you begin to imagine the joyful realisation of glory in that moment, along with all the time in the universe to enjoy it? It's unbelievably exciting!

We have not yet finished with Paul's verse to the Corinthians. There is still more in our 'priceless inheritance'.

Take it further

- How could our 'confident hope' of future glory help to relieve the temporary burdens of:

  – Low self-esteem?
  – Defeats and disappointments?
  – Poverty and lack?

Take it to Jesus

Jesus, help me to see all that is coming to me in the 'priceless inheritance', so that I would not derive my sense of worth and value from here alone. Teach me at my strongest to be humble, and at my weakest to be confident because You are strong and living in me. Give me peace and mercy to handle any suffering that may come my way, and keep the hope of a glorious resurrection at the forefront of my mind.
Amen.

Strength will replace frailty, durability will replace debility, weakness will be replaced with great power. The brief spell of youthfulness we experience *here* will be our continual state *there*, but even better.

8
Unbeatable Strength

They are buried in weakness, but they will be
raised in strength.
1 Corinthians 15:43

The third 'priceless inheritance' of the resurrection is
unbeatable *strength*.

Could it be that Superman's extraordinary strength had
been removed by the dangerous molecule chamber? It
appeared to Lex Luther and his alien partners that his
powers had finally been stripped away. They thought he
was now just human. He knelt before General Zod (back
when bad-guy names were truly legendary) who
demanded he take his hand and swear loyalty. But, of
course, Superman was as strong as ever – the molecule
chamber could not harm him! Instead of surrendering to
the hand of the enemy, he crushed it with his superhero
strength and threw him into the icy abyss![33]

---

[33] *Superman II*. Distributed by Warner Bros, 1980.

Sorry if I just spoilt the end of *Superman II* for you! I will always remember watching it as a child of the 1980s. This comic-book legend began a genre that is now one of the most popular in movie history. Now there are superheroes everywhere. I think one of the reasons we love watching superhero movies is because deep down we have a profound desire to replace our weakness with strength. We want the strength to be better than ordinary. We want the strength to remove impossible obstacles, make things happen faster, fly above the clouds – the list goes on. These ideas of strength are a dream in comparison to our limitations.

This third promise is that we will take on strength we only dream of today. We will become unbeatable.

The chiropractor dug his thumb into my hip, and I winced. The days of being young and fit felt like a distant memory. I had only pulled a muscle, but I had felt its pain for the last year. That's right – a whole year. My mind wandered to the good old days where I could pull muscles every weekend and still mix it with the best of them. I was unbeatable back then. (OK, maybe my memories are a little rose-tinted.)

It was clear to me that my body was not what it used to be. The slightly discouraging feeling of being weaker takes some embracing. But while my mirror and my experience may disagree, the human body is an absolute marvel. Science has discovered some amazing facts about us. Did you know that if you took all the telephones on the planet and added up all their electrical impulses, your brain would still create more? And in the time it takes to read this fact, 50,000 cells in your body just died and got replaced with new cells? Or that your eye can register 10 million different colours?[34]

Yet, with all this and more glory in our wiring, most would not deny our weakness. We get sick all too easily, our muscles ache at the thought of walking to the shops and our minds are susceptible to seasons of depression. Ultimately, our bodies age and age until they cease to function at all. They are, as Paul describes, 'buried in weakness', meaning that along with being dishonourable, our final moments are our absolute weakest. Unlike superheroes, we succumb to mortality.

The transformation in our resurrection, then, could not be starker than here. Paul is saying that we will be raised from our weakest possible moment into a place of unbeatable strength. This strength will replace frailty, durability will replace debility, weakness will be replaced with great power. The brief spell of youthfulness we experience *here* will be our continual state *there*, but even better.

This new body will not get sick, or diseased, or depressed. The promise of strength is a promise of health. Our body *here* is fit for a few years. Our body *there* will be fit for eternity. It will not age and succumb to death any more. It will not yield to lusts and be weak in the way that we are now when presented with temptation.

The strength we all desire will be given to us in fullness. You can't buy that *here*.

---

[34] brightside.me/article/100-quick-and-fascinating-facts-about-the-human-body-38305 (accessed 16th April 2021).

This is a great hope to those of us experiencing weakness today. The Bible reminds us:

> That is why we never give up. Though our bodies are dying, our spirits are being renewed every day. For our present troubles are small and won't last very long. Yet they produce for us a glory that vastly outweighs them and will last forever! So we don't look at the troubles we can see now; rather, we fix our gaze on things that cannot be seen. For the things we see now will soon be gone, but the things we cannot see will last forever.
>
> *2 Corinthians 4:16-18*

This tells us that we will not be weak for long. You may be losing strengths you once had, but you do not need to lose that inner strength and ability to respond with hopeful faith. It's a truth that the world can take everything from you except your ability to choose how you respond. We can choose to put our weaknesses, as Paul did, into the context of faith – where anything is possible. God can be glorified through their healing, or through our hopefulness despite them. Either way we are not losing, we are overcoming, because in spirit we are already unbeatable – and one day our bodies will catch up with the fact.

Take it further

- Until we receive this unbeatable strength, the Bible encourages us to depend on God: 'A final word: Be strong in the Lord and in his mighty power' (Ephesians 6:10). What do you think this means?

- 2 Corinthians 4:18 tells us that what we focus on is the key: 'So we don't look at the troubles we can see now; rather, we fix our gaze on things that cannot be seen.' This takes practice. Perhaps start by imagining you are sitting somewhere you love with Jesus, and then mentally bring Jesus into the middle of whatever troubles you are experiencing now, and focus on Him. What is He saying to you about them?

Take it to Jesus

Jesus, help me to fix my eyes and thoughts on the unseen and eternal when I'm tempted to think only of now. Where I experience weakness, help me to find my strength in You. Though my body may be weary with weakness, let my spirit rise every day with the power to overcome every negative and despairing thought. Remind me that I can do all things with You[35] and have everything I could ever need for this day.
Amen.

---

[35] See Philippians 4:13.

We will not wrestle with ourselves to do the right thing or experience the constant pull of our flesh to be someone we are not. We will not need a public face to hide a private reality. We will be truly and permanently whole.

9
Unearthly Bodies

For we know that when this earthly tent we live in is taken down (that is, when we die and leave this earthly body), we will have a house in heaven, an eternal body made for us by God himself and not by human hands. We grow weary in our present bodies, and we long to put on our heavenly bodies like new clothing. For we will put on heavenly bodies; we will not be spirits without bodies. While we live in these earthly bodies, we groan and sigh, but it's not that we want to die and get rid of these bodies that clothe us. Rather, we want to put on our new bodies so that these dying bodies will be swallowed up by life. God himself has prepared us for this, and as a guarantee he has given us his Holy Spirit.
2 Corinthians 5:1-5

The fourth 'priceless inheritance' of the resurrection is a *spiritual* body – like nothing on earth.

I had the misfortune to fall off a ladder last year. I was several steps up, sanding a window frame. The top window was held open by a long metal arm, allowing me to hold on to the frame itself with one hand while I sanded with the other. It was a problem, then, when I accidentally hit the metal arm with the sander. It popped off its hook and the previously open window slammed on to the fingers of my left hand, sending me backwards in a jolt of pain. This movement caused the stepladder to topple. In a flash, I was falling without any grace or any hope of righting myself to land feet first. I hit the wooden floor on my side, hard. I gasped for breath while holding my fingers. After finding my breath again, I tried to get up but realised my chest pain wouldn't allow me to move very much at all – and my knee hurt badly. I was a mess.

A thorough check-up revealed I had some bruised and cracked ribs, a bruised knee and a slightly bruised ego to match. My falling scream was apparently a bit high pitched. I learned that day that my body cannot deny physics. Gravity and solid things will win out over my flesh and bones every time.

And yet this wasn't so for Jesus.

Scholars have marvelled over the resurrection body of Jesus Christ as revealed in Luke 24:36-43 and John 20:19-20. Here's Luke's account, followed by John's:

> While they were still talking about this, Jesus himself stood among them and said to them, 'Peace be with you.'

They were startled and frightened, thinking they saw a ghost. He said to them, 'Why are you troubled, and why do doubts rise in your minds? Look at my hands and my feet. It is I myself! Touch me and see; a ghost does not have flesh and bones, as you see I have.'

When he had said this, he showed them his hands and feet. And while they still did not believe it because of joy and amazement, he asked them, 'Do you have anything here to eat?' They gave him a piece of broiled fish, and he took it and ate it in their presence.

(NIV)

On the evening of that first day of the week, when the disciples were together, with the doors locked for fear of the Jewish leaders, Jesus came and stood among them and said, 'Peace be with you!' After he said this, he showed them his hands and side.

(NIV)

Did you see it? His resurrected body was perfectly physical *and* spiritual in nature.

He was able to appear among them while doors were locked, according to John, and yet the disciples could touch Him and see that He had flesh and bones in Luke's account. Could it be that He moved through solid walls or wooden doors? That's the unavoidable implication. When this new 'spiritual body' encounters physics, it's the physics that bend and move.

Some might think about heaven as a purely spiritual existence, floating on the clouds and escaping the limitations of our bodies. On the other hand, atheists believe all that exists is the material world and there is no 'spiritual' realm at all, only an end to things. In Jesus, we see a powerful combination of both the material and spiritual in one body. He was neither a ghost nor a human in the conventional sense. He had a body like we have never experienced, and it is an archetype for our future bodies.[36]

What's especially encouraging to me is that He wanted to eat breakfast! These observations give us some clues about the kind of body Paul is talking about when he says that we will be 'buried as natural … bodies' and 'raised as spiritual bodies'.[37]

It answers questions such as, 'Will we have actual bodies?' Yes, we will.

Will we live in a physical reality as we do now? Yes, we will.

Will we be able to eat great food? The best.

Drink wine? If it takes your fancy.

More than these things, it appears we may have some cool spiritual abilities to boot. We are dipping into an area of great mystery again here, but I think it's safe to say that we are not even close to tapping into the potential these new bodies will have.

Furthermore, we will be spiritual in every sense. *Here* we are dominated by the corrupt senses, drives and appetites of our human nature, which is why we struggle with sin. God has given us 'a deposit, guaranteeing what is to come' – the presence of the Spirit to guide and

---

[36] Wright, *Surprised by Hope*, p149.

[37] 1 Corinthians 15:44.

empower us.[38] But this future, spiritual body will be completely spiritually dominated. It will meet our profound desire for complete integrity. We will not wrestle with ourselves to do the right thing or experience the constant pull of our flesh to be someone we are not. We will not need a public face to hide a private reality. We will be truly and permanently whole. Yes, our earthly body is only good for a short time, but the spiritual body is designed for eternal life and no other existence matches it.

Paul has painted his four-line response in 1 Corinthians 15:42-44 as an absolutely priceless picture for us to look forward to. On top of living in paradise under the peaceful rule and reign of Christ, we will have the time, happiness, strength and integrity we yearn for. This is our great expectation. It's an inheritance that causes all the jewels in the Tower of London to pale in comparison.

> And now, dear brothers and sisters, we want you to know what will happen to the believers who have died so you will not grieve like people who have no hope. For since we believe that Jesus died and was raised to life again, we also believe that when Jesus returns, God will bring back with him the believers who have died.
> *1 Thessalonians 4:13-14*

Try to imagine the moment we are raised or transformed and become fully aware of these new realities. The

---

[38] 2 Corinthians 1:22, NIV.

combined excitement of unlimited time, unbelievable glory, unbeatable strength and unearthly bodies will fill us with an overwhelming joy like we have never imagined, and on top of all this, we will be reunited with those we lost who also died in Christ's promise of resurrection. We will experience the overwhelming happiness of seeing faces we love once again, with paradise as the backdrop of an exciting future, and the presence of Jesus, the One who made it all possible, all around us. Believe me, this day is going to inspire the greatest party the universe has ever seen.

I may even break with a well-established practice and join you on the dance floor, if my new body has abilities this one has clearly lost.

Take it further

- Reflect: How does this 'priceless inheritance' change the way we view this life now?

- Picturing the day when we receive these new realities is an important part of hoping. Take a moment in prayer to place yourself in the day this 'priceless inheritance' becomes a reality. Meditate on each aspect of the inheritance and absorb its truth into your spirit. You may be able to consider people you will see again.

Take it to Jesus

Jesus, help me to break free of the dictates of my old self, and live by Your Spirit. I want to be more and more under Your control. Teach me what it means to be faithful to You here, so that I can receive my reward there. Open the eyes of my spirit to see the day I'm hoping for – the day I am present and united completely with You, reunited with my loved ones, the day I receive my 'priceless inheritance' and am awakened to paradise. Let this picture always be the lens through which I see my future.
Amen.

Our hope is that on this day we will receive honour from our heavenly Father. You think you have any confidence now? Wait until after this moment.

10
Rewarding the Faithful

Anyone who builds on that foundation may use
a variety of materials – gold, silver, jewels, wood,
hay, or straw. But on the judgment day, fire will
reveal what kind of work each builder has done.
The fire will show if a person's work has any
value. If the work survives, that builder will
receive a reward. But if the work is burned up,
the builder will suffer great loss. The builder will
be saved, but like someone barely escaping
through a wall of flames.
1 Corinthians 3:12-15

'Not good enough.'

I had just handed in my best piece of artwork and this
was the teacher's response. I was incensed. How could
they make such a judgement? Perhaps I was consigned to
join the number of artists who were only appreciated after
they had died. Or perhaps it was, in fact, rubbish.

What got to me – and still does, if I'm honest – was that this was a class in modern art in the mid-1990s. Now, forgive me if you're reading this and you're an artist or a fan of modern art, but I had just been on a trip to London where the central piece of artwork in the gallery was made of some hospital beds piled on top of one another. People were wowed by the vision of the artist. I saw a waste of time and beds.

This was modern art, as far as I could tell. You could get away with pretty much anything, but only if you had a 'name'. My ego was even more bruised because my piece of work was a failure in an era of 'art' where you could pretty much paint a red square and be regarded as a genius.[39] How could I possibly fail?

Our verse above suggests a day *there* when all our work as Christians will be subject to a judgement, to see if it has any value. Will it have been the artistry of faithful obedience? Or an expression of whatever we could get away with? Will it pass the test of purity? Or will it be found to be corrupted by selfish ambition?

It's important to note from the outset that the purpose of this judgement is not to decide if we were good enough to enter heaven. That is decided in the moment we choose to trust in Jesus for our salvation. No, rather this day has to do with God finding any reason He can to bless us. That's His preference, anyway. We know this because He's looking at the small things, not only the big.

[39] Source: www.kazimirmalevich.org/red-square (accessed 4th June 2021).

And if you give even a cup of cold water to one
of the least of my followers, you will surely be
rewarded.
Matthew 10:42

He should not be seen like an angry judge, looking for a
reason to punish us, but as a Father looking to reward us
because He's proud of us. What might these rewards look
like?

Honour that promotes us

Anyone who wants to serve me must follow me,
because my servants must be where I am. And
the Father will honor anyone who serves me.
John 12:26

To be honoured is a wonderful thing. When others speak
highly of us, it lifts our spirits and emboldens our work
even further. It gives us greater confidence to be ourselves.
Our hope is that on this day we will receive honour from
our heavenly Father. You think you have any confidence
now? Wait until after this moment. We will be brimming
with every kind of positive emotion on the day God points
out every individual act worthy of honour. 'Look at when
you did *this*…' He will say, 'and I was so proud when you
did *that*. In *this* moment you really showed me your faith;
in *that* moment you got the angels clapping.' Yes, this will
be an incredible occasion for us, and perhaps a surprising
one also. Jesus taught that:

> Many who are the greatest now will be least
> important then, and those who seem least
> important now will be the greatest then.
> *Matthew 19:30*

Honour will promote many who were considered small or insignificant in this life, or whose faith, good works and acts of obedience weren't as obvious to us as they were to God. It seems clear that we will not all come through with the same amount of honour. Honour *there* will be the just reward of faithfulness *here*.

Responsibilities that fit us

> The master was full of praise. 'Well done, my
> good and faithful servant. You have been
> faithful in handling this small amount, so now I
> will give you many more responsibilities. Let's
> celebrate together!'
> *Matthew 25:21*

Jesus uttered these words during what is known as the 'parable of the three servants'. In it, Jesus described a master leaving his three servants with differing bags of silver, and then returning one day to see what they had made of the investment. This verse shows his response to the servant who took his investment and handled it wisely. It begins with affirmation but doesn't stop there – it speaks of many more responsibilities. You might think, 'Great, thanks, Jesus, but I wanted to get to heaven and put my feet up!'

I think it's reasonable to assume that life *there* won't just be a continual holiday. Work is part of our DNA. We need it. We will all work in an area of gifting and purpose that will bring real meaning and energy to our lives. Work won't know the seasons of toiling and sweating with little to no thanks, reward or accomplishment. Working on the new earth will always be a matter of joy, rather than pain.[40] We will have differing levels of responsibility and this parable suggests that our responsibilities, far from being a heavy burden, will be a great privilege and reward tied to our faithfulness *here*, and a great reason for a celebration with Him.

A new name that defines us

> To everyone who is victorious I will give … a white stone, and on the stone will be engraved a new name that no one understands except the one who receives it.
> *Revelation 2:17*

Names can carry meaning. My name, Michael, means 'Who is like God?', or so I heard. It has little impact on my self-esteem, as it seems to be a rhetorical question – also, I can think of every way in which I am very much not 'like God'. The idea here in Revelation, though, is that as a reward for overcoming, we will be defined forever in a new way and this definition will resonate very deeply with us.

---

[40] See Genesis 3:17-19, where humankind's fall into sin results in a negative change to our experience of 'working' in the earth.

Perhaps, just as adopted children take on a new name legally, this moment will ceremonially establish our new identity. I imagine it will be a moment of great honour and healing for the soul, affirming our absolute salvation from everything that went before. Perhaps in life we felt the pain of great regret, and on this day God hands us a glorious white stone with the name inscribed 'free'. Perhaps we experienced abuse, and the stone says we are 'whole'. Maybe the name finally undoes the harmful labels others have given us in life. Whatever is written, this verse tells us that we will understand *why* it was uniquely given to us. It will be a defining moment of reward.

Crowns that adorn us

> And now the prize awaits me – the crown of righteousness, which the Lord, the righteous Judge, will give me on the day of his return. And the prize is not just for me but for all who eagerly look forward to his appearing.
> *2 Timothy 4:8*

Crowns are made to adorn royalty. To set them above and beyond the ordinary. They beautify a person in a way caps, hats and wigs never will. The hope Paul expresses here to Timothy is that one day he will receive a beautiful 'crown of righteousness'. Righteousness will add the golden factor to our lives *there*.

There are other crowns too. James mentions the 'crown of life'; Peter talks of the crown of 'never-ending glory and honor'.[41] And the book of Revelation describes an event where significant characters in the throne room of God lay down their 'crowns' before Him and the One who bore the crown of thorns so that we could get *there*.[42]

What a beautiful moment.

There's a challenge in this chapter, of course. The judgement could find us wanting to some degree. Paul suggests that while *we* will survive the test, our work for Jesus may not. If we treat God's kingdom like a route to fame and earthly glory, or compromise our faithfulness to His calling, we will likely experience a sense of loss on that day – loss because we could have been so much more. We could have painted the *Mona Lisa* of service with our lives, but instead we settled with all the effort it takes to paint a red square.

Make no mistake, this will be a great day. He's going to be giving out gifts, rewarding faithfulness and imparting new purpose everywhere and to everyone. We will revel in the honour He bestows, be excited by the responsibilities He's prepared, be astounded by the way He defines us and rejoice at the crowns He has placed upon us.

May we look forward to the day He says to us, 'Well done, my good and faithful servant.'

---

[41] James 1:12; 1 Peter 5:4.

[42] Revelation 4:10-11.

Take it further

- Reflect on how are you currently serving Jesus, and why.

- What could you do to ensure you are doing your best with the talents and opportunities invested in you?

Take it to Jesus

Jesus, I long to hear those words, 'Well done, my good and faithful servant.' Teach me to respond to Your calling upon my life with faithful obedience and urgency. Show me where I can serve You today. Reveal the purpose for which You created me, and my place in Your body – the Church. Empower me with Your strength so that I am able to carry what You want me to carry. Open my eyes to new opportunities and reorder my priorities so that I can be found doing the work that lasts.
Amen.

We will all – single in this life, or married – be more fulfilled *there* than we are *here*, in a new kind of union.

11
Like the Angels

For when the dead rise, they will neither marry
nor be given in marriage. In this respect they will
be like the angels in heaven.
Mark 12:25

She said yes.

I was so happy the day my wife agreed to be my wife.
I knew she liked me, but I still loaded the odds of her
saying yes in my favour. Knowing her love of animals,
especially little furry cute ones, I bought a kitten. This
kitten wasn't just any kitten. It was the cutest kitten I could
find online. I tied the engagement ring to a ribbon around
the kitten's neck, being careful not to squeeze too tightly,
and hid him in the bathroom until she arrived at my flat.

That evening, I opened the bathroom door just enough
for Edward (she named him) to get the chance to wander
around the flat, and hopefully into the living room, where
I hoped we would be busy kissing and watching TV. It
turned out we were watching TV.

And sure enough, in he walked.

I'm not sure what surprised her more. The moment she saw the kitten, or the next moment when I was on bended knee asking her to take the ring and marry me. In retrospect, the kitten took the limelight and the attention away from what I had dreamed would be the golden moment. But the good news is, she said yes. My £25 on a ball of fluff was well spent. In 2011, I had the privilege of marrying this amazing girl.

But hang on, what did Jesus just say?

Jesus is answering a question from the Sadducees, who are trying to discredit the notion of the resurrection by suggesting that people who have had more than one marriage would be in the preposterous position of having to choose between spouses on the other side. Surely this would be unimaginably difficult and unloving, resulting in some early heartbreak on one's arrival *there*, right? Either that or there are multi-person marriages in heaven.

Jesus responds with this simple and most intriguing answer. There will be no marriage in heaven, and in this way, we will 'be like the angels'.

What are we to make of this answer?

Is Jesus teaching that those of us who live in marriages will be split up? That sex will no longer be part of life? That I wasted my money on the kitten? Do our present intimate relationships simply come to an end, because there is no need of them any more? The implications are far reaching and have been the source of much debate.

To at least try to answer the question, let's look at marriage in the Bible.

> Then the LORD God made a woman from the rib,
> and he brought her to the man.

'At last!' the man exclaimed.
'This one is bone from my bone,
and flesh from my flesh!
She will be called "woman,"
because she was taken from 'man.'"

This explains why a man leaves his father and mother and is joined to his wife, and the two are united into one.

Genesis 2:22-24

The first mention of marriage comes hot on the heels of creation. It's not a modern invention but sourced at the very beginning of the Bible. It describes the wonderful mystery of union between a man and woman. Union means that two can return to the state of being one, just as if the rib had never left the cage.

This idea of union is also found in God Himself, whom the Scriptures reveal as three persons – Father, Son and Spirit, existing as one and in whose image we were created.[43] Before marriage is anything else, it is union. It communicates to us that perfect unity between distinct persons with their own centres of consciousness, identity and personality is possible, and not just possible, but the direction of all God's design. Jesus expressed this idea in His prayer for us:

I pray that they will all be one, just as you and I are one – as you are in me, Father, and I am in you.
John 17:21

---

[43] See Genesis 1:27.

This union is confirmed in the covenant, or promise, we make to one another, followed by sexual union where two literally become one body. The promise creates trust, and trust leads to vulnerability of the deepest kind. Pleasure and new life are the overflow of this amazing union.

God's goal in creation is that we reflect His image, and included in His image is perfect union between distinct persons. In this age, marriage has been given to us as one way of achieving this purpose. It appears, from Jesus' words, that marriage will not be required for this union to be possible in the next.

I've already suggested that there will be some degree of continuity in paradise. God isn't scrapping everything and beginning again with an entirely different kind of existence. Relationships will continue, but in a far richer experience of them. The resurrection accounts of Jesus strongly imply that we will still be joined by our experiences in this age; we will not suddenly lose all memory of one another. Union will still be beautiful and rewarding and fun, because that's who God is and always will be. Perhaps in the absence of sin we will no longer need a 'promise' of faithfulness? We will just be faithful. Without the culture driving us towards selfish behaviour, we will be selfless. Without greed we will be satisfied, without lust we will be pure. Who knows, perhaps God has something altogether better than marriage awaiting us?

Will there be sex on the new earth, and will we create new people? No one can answer this question definitively because the Bible is unclear. That leaves us with speculations, and we cannot build any kind of confident theology upon them. Jesus could be implying that we will 'be like the angels' in that there is a fixed number of them, and they are not multiplying.

Alternatively, human life may continue to abound and multiply, just as it was designed to, in whatever intimacy replaces marriage. I'm not aware of a definitive verse suggesting life creation would suddenly cease. Childbearing is painful because of sin,[44] but in new bodies this could be very different, and as it was intended before the Fall. And if it were possible, we can only speculate as to where all these new people would live.

While it's not wrong to imagine a little, let's remember what we do know. If in heaven, marriage isn't the way we experience the union we were made for, then you can be sure that what God does have for us will be 'better by far'.[45] Those of us who married will not wander around heaven missing anything, as if God had robbed us of a limb. We will all – single in this life, or married – be more fulfilled *there* than we are *here*, in a new kind of union. Jesus' response to the dilemma of the Sadducees suggests that whatever God has prepared will also resolve any potential conflict in the event we have been married more than once.

So our perspective in the mystery should be one of faith, trusting that what God has prepared for our relationships will be an improvement, not a diminishment.

---

[44] See Genesis 3:16.
[45] Philippians 1:23, NIV.

> Let us be glad and rejoice,
> and let us give honor to him.
> For the time has come for the wedding feast of
> the Lamb,
> and his bride has prepared herself.
> *Revelation 19:7*

We should see marriage as less of a destination and more of a signpost. A signpost that reminds us that God is all about union, the union He already has within Himself, the union He created us for with each other, and His desire for perfect union with us.

Marriage is a signpost towards the greatest reunion of all – not the rib returning to the cage, but people returning to their creator. Jesus calls Himself the 'groom', and the 'bride' is His Church.[46] One of the first things we will do when we get *there*, is participate in a huge wedding party. We will no longer be 'engaged', we will be fully His, and He will be fully ours, and this union will be the source of our greatest joy.

---

[46] Luke 5:35; Revelation 19:7.

Take it further

- Married? What is God saying to you about the priority for your marriage in this season? How might you improve on your union?

- Single? Friendship with God and others build union into your life. Who are you investing in now that is already, or could become, a vital source of union and support for you?

- Both: What are the implications of a biblical view of marriage for our culture today?

Take it to Jesus

Jesus, I am reminded that union is Your passion. You came to me when I was divorced from You and You died to make union with me possible. Help me to not take this for granted today. I want to live in the intimacy of this union with You so that the love and peace of that union would overflow into every area of my life. I want what You prayed for, to be one with others in your body, the Church. Help me to invest wisely and generously into all these relationships in my life.

Amen.

Because Jesus is 'the resurrection and the life', we can be certain that on the day death comes calling, His voice will shout louder. He will shout 'life' at just the right time, before death can get its hands on us.

12
Two Words and Three Letters

I have hidden your word in my heart.
Psalm 119:11

Once I crashed a van into a wall.

As a part-time newspaper courier, I only had one job: get the papers to the shops before dawn. However, on this fateful Saturday morning, I failed. Distracted by thoughts of my bed, I took my eyes off the road in front of me for a few moments while driving at the national speed limit. When they returned to the windscreen, instead of a road sprawling out before me I could only see the wall of a bridge seconds in front of me. I had inadvertently nudged the steering wheel off course.

I don't remember much about that moment, but I do remember uttering the word, 'JESUSSSS!' Now, I'm not accustomed to swearing often, and if you're reading this and you're my mother, then never. But when I said 'JESUSSSS!' it was not in the cursing sense. His name was the first word that rose to the surface when my life flashed before my eyes, and I had no clue if I would survive to tell the tale. Somewhere deep within me I knew the word I needed to call upon when it mattered.

Now, I did survive, quite miraculously. There was little left of the van, or indeed the wall that I hit, but I walked away with only a few minor injuries – and an unmistakable answer to a momentary cry for help.

You see, when the moment of fear comes, what's *in* you is what will come out. The things we believe deeply are important because they shape our response mechanism when all we can see is the end of the road. The psalmist encourages us to hide God's word in our hearts, so that faith rises in us just when we need it most.

And the first two words you need to know deeply are 'I am':

> But now, as to whether there will be a resurrection of the dead – haven't you ever read about this in the Scriptures? Long after Abraham, Isaac, and Jacob had died, God said, 'I am the God of Abraham, the God of Isaac, and the God of Jacob.' So he is the God of the living, not the dead.
> *Matthew 22:31-32*

It's easy to miss the genius in Jesus' response to the Sadducees – a sect of Judaism that had concluded by studying the first five books of the Hebrew Scriptures (the Torah) that there was *no* resurrection. Armed with watertight arguments that had likely been formed, debated and defended by the most educated of teachers, these unfortunate men decided to pick on Jesus one day to test Him on His view on living after dying.

Jesus pointed out that the Torah uses the present tense, 'I am', not the past tense, 'I was', when describing God's relationship to Abraham, Isaac and Jacob. According to Jesus' teaching, these ancient heroes of the faith are alive and well, right now. Luke confirms this in his record of the same conversation, adding a few words: 'So he is the God of the living, not the dead, for they are all alive to him'.[47]

This was profoundly amazing. He just untangled years of intellectual debate with two words and three letters: 'I am'. And if you know your Bible, there was something else going on under the surface here. Jesus was establishing His own identity as God. He was setting people up to see that He is the 'I am' in the flesh. In case you had any doubt on the matter, Jesus clearly taught that there *is* life beyond dying, and He is right at the heart of it.

Another conversation, recorded in Mark 14:28, confirms Jesus' grip on absolute resurrection confidence: 'But after I am raised from the dead, I will go ahead of you to Galilee and meet you there.' Talk about forward planning. Jesus, not yet crucified, was informing the disciples of His plans and whereabouts after His resurrection! His diary extended beyond the grave, His to-do list beyond the small matter of His dying.

A woman called Martha was involved in one of the greatest conversations recorded between Jesus and a person (in my opinion), and it began with the same two words and three letters that even a Jewish scholar could easily miss.

---

[47] Luke 20:38.

> Jesus told her, 'I am the resurrection and the life. Anyone who believes in me will live, even after dying.'
> *John 11:25*

Breathe on that a moment. '*I am* the resurrection and the life.'

He wasn't pointing to any other answer to the problem of death than Himself. Because He rises, we can rise. Because He is life, we can live.[48] He confirmed this identity again when he said:

> I am the way, the truth, and the life. No one can come to the Father except through me.
> *John 14:6*

See it? There it is again: 'I am'. The key to our being rock-solid certain about *there* is being rock-solid certain about who Jesus is. Our believing in Him is the great doorway to the 'confident hope' we read about earlier in Colossians 1:4-5.

> Say this to the people of Israel: I AM has sent me to you.
> *Exodus 3:14*

The third chapter of Exodus also tells us that God revealed Himself as 'I am'. After 400 years of slavery in Egypt, God showed up in a burning bush to call Moses into leadership. When Moses asked God what he should say to

---

48 See John 14:19.

the Hebrews when they asked about who sent him to lead them, God responded with those two words: 'I AM'.

On the face of it, this may seem like a strange answer. It helps to boil 'I am' down to its meaning in essence. The word in Hebrew is *ehyeh* and it's a powerful statement of self-existence. It means that God's existence isn't contingent on anything or anyone else. He *is* life. No one gives life to Him. It can also mean He is very present and able to accomplish anything He wants.

Now, imagine if you haven't heard from God for centuries and you're living on stories handed down from one generation to the next. 'I exist' in that context is a powerful moment of revelation, right? To a people desperate for hope, 'I am' would have told them everything they needed to know.

'I am' is everything we need to know. It's where faith begins and hope is birthed. Trusting in Jesus as the self-existent author of life is the foundation of hope in the face of dying.

Back to Martha. Jesus is asking her the crucial question – do you believe deep down in your heart that 'I am'? He knows this deep trust in Him will be the difference between 'confident hope' and debilitating fear in the face of dying. Her answer is yes!

I think there's a truth for us here that is worth reflecting on. The degree to which you and I trust in Jesus Christ – the 'I am' – will correspond with the strength of our hope. It's possible that our fears expose the fact that we don't *really* trust Him. We think we do, and perhaps we say we do, but if fear and worry and holding on to this life are our dominant preoccupations, they betray our lack of

113

confidence, revealing that what we believe deeply is something else.

Uncertainties create the conditions for fear to reign. Uprooting uncertainties and replacing them with Jesus' words will transform your view of the future and the way you cope with *here*. Jesus comforts the anxious Martha with more words worth hiding in your heart: 'Everyone who lives in me and believes in me will never ever die.'[49]

Contrary to what some people say, faith is not an exercise in wishing – it can be robust, built on multiple layers of knowledge and reason and experience. The more knowledge and experience, the stronger the faith; the more faith, the more certain we become. And it goes without saying that the more certain we are, the less uncertainty can rule our hearts with fear.

Hebrews 11:1 tells us that 'faith is the assurance of things hoped for, the conviction of things not seen' (ESV). Physicist Peter Higgs had a belief that the Higgs boson particle existed before he saw it in the Large Hadron Collider, because it was evident to him by its effect on the visible world of physics.[50] Likewise, the things we cannot see can be understood with a certain faith if we have enough evidence for them in the 'effects' we see around us.

There are convincing proofs across philosophy, history and the sciences that powerfully support the existence of an intelligent and personal creator, the reliability of the Bible and the claims Jesus made about Himself. His 'effect'

[49] John 11:26.
[50] Source home.cern/science/physics/higgs-boson (accessed 8th September 2021).

is everywhere, if you are willing to examine the combination of all three. Laid alongside current naturalistic theories, they appear far more reasonable to me. But it's His own resurrection that provides one of the greatest evidences and separates Him from every other claim or religion, and it's worth us observing these effects here, before we move on.

1. Jesus definitely died. We know this fact because the Bible describes blood and water flowing out as a result of the spear in His side,[51] a process that happens as a result of hypovolemic shock, as the body effectively shuts down with low blood pressure. The claim that He got very close to death but then recovered – after a Roman flogging and crucifixion, and in just three days – requires even more faith.

2. Jesus' tomb contained no body. Popular theory says that the disciples must have stolen it to make it look like a resurrection happened. But this theory has problems. This wasn't a grave in a public cemetery; it was a tomb guarded by Roman soldiers.[52] Stealing the body would be no easy task to accomplish. If they did manage it, when they were later arrested and threatened with death for the claim of resurrection, it's more likely they would have delivered the body than continued to defend a lie.[53]

---

[51] See John 19:34.

[52] See Matthew 27:62-66.

[53] Source: www.biola.edu/blogs/biola-magazine/2013/did-the-apostles-really-die-as-martyrs-for-their-f (accessed 2nd June 2021).

3. All the disciples and around 500 others who saw Him following His resurrection[54] were completely convinced that they had been with the risen Jesus – many were convinced enough to die for this belief. Hallucinations don't happen to this many people, and they don't give up their lives for something they're not certain about. The resurrection makes sense of this conviction.

4. The effect on the early Church is extraordinary. The disciples literally moved from sorrow and despair to dynamic influencers leading a movement that impacted a nation within weeks. Something ground-breaking happened to create such a transformation in them and in the region. Within 300 years, the Roman Empire that crucified Jesus was Christian. The resurrection explains the fact that ordinary men and women effected such a huge change in the world then and to this day.[55]

No good counter claim has been produced to explain these evidences away in 2,000 years. That is quite something! Added to my own personal experience of Jesus as a

---

[54] See 1 Corinthians 15:6.

[55] My paraphrase of the four evidences. Sources include: www.reasonablefaith.org/writings/popular-writings/jesus-of-nazareth/the-resurrection-of-jesus (accessed 30th December 2020). stevenruff.com/2021/04/06/false-theories-of-the-resurrection-part-2-why-the-swoon-theory-comes-up-short (accessed 8th September 2021); bible.org/article/false-theories-against-resurrection-christ (accessed 8th September 2021).

tangible presence and friend in my life, I for one am certain Jesus really is 'the resurrection and the life'.

And if Jesus rose from the dead, then living after dying is possible for all of us.

I grew up with a real fear of death. My imagination would run wild as a child. I never understood it until years later, but I would experience panic attacks and long periods of anxiety. I remember once hearing a local news story about a flesh-eating disease that would kill within forty-eight hours. That night I lay in bed unable to sleep because every itch and twitch made me more and more convinced I had contracted the bacteria. I was a hypochondriac without a clue about how to stop worrying about the unknown.

In my teens I knew I needed help. The thing that really changed everything for me was that I came to discover the near 'I am' presence of God in moments of simple worship in my room. In moments of intimate prayer, He gave me enough peace and strength to meet each day's need; the Holy Spirit met with me there and turned my panic stations into rooms for His holy, peaceful presence. My mental health improved because my spiritual health improved. Through opening myself up to prayer, and from that place of prayer, studying the Scriptures, I found many of the truths that now act as guards around my mind. Truth set me free from the lies and half-truths I had so easily accepted before. As I hid the word in my heart,[56] my trust in Jesus grew.

Jesus is more than a concept, you see. He is a living person who promises to show up through His Spirit if we

[56] See Psalm 119:11.

desire to encounter Him. If we make time to know the Spirit, we will find that we really come to know Jesus. This powerful *experience* built on the foundation of *reason* has had a transformative effect on me and countless others across the world, and He can meet you too.

So allow me to ask you a question: Do *you* believe He is 'the resurrection and the life'? And another: Are you living in panic stations, or in rooms of His holy, peaceful presence?

> God raised him up, loosing the pangs of death, because it was not possible for him to be held by it.
> *Acts 2:24 (ESV)*

I love this verse. What's true for Jesus will be true for you and me. It is just not possible for death to hold on to you.

My son is three and a half and can shout so loud the whole street must wake up. Usually, just before dawn, while I am sound asleep in the comfort of my bed, his 'I-need-a-wee-wee' shout comes as quite a rude awakening. Suddenly I sit bolt upright and jump out of bed, and the morning routine has begun.

Because Jesus is 'the resurrection and the life', we can be certain that on the day death comes calling, His voice will shout louder. He will shout 'life' at just the right time, before death can get its hands on us. At His command we will live along with Abraham, Isaac, Jacob and everyone who has died looking to Jesus Christ, the life-giver. Just as Martha discovered, we will not spend one more second in its darkness than He allows – we will *never* die.

If we're awake when that moment comes, what's *in* us is what will rise to the surface. My prayer is that the Holy Spirit plants this certain faith so deeply within us that, rather than calling His name in fear or confusion, it results in the adoration of Jesus as we see Him calling us home.

You see, this 'confident hope' of ours is built on something rock solid: two words and three letters.

Take it further

- Read Psalm 119:11. What could you do practically to ensure you have hidden His word in your heart?

- What comes out of you when you're faced with a crisis or challenge? Fear or faith?

Take it to Jesus

Jesus, I want to be rock solid in my belief in You and Your every word. Let Your words penetrate my heart, renew my mind and increase my faith so that they result in a 'confident hope'. I want faith to be my response mechanism to everything in life, and I know that treasuring Your words is the key to this. Help me to overcome the fear of death by seeing that You have complete victory over it and can meet me there and walk me safely through to the other side. I place myself again in the hands of the One who is 'the resurrection and the life'. Amen.

Surrendering with faith opens the door to complete forgiveness and restoration of our relationship with God. Jesus makes all this possible because He first surrendered His life for us.

13
What About Hell?

For this is how God loved the world: He gave his
one and only Son, so that everyone who
believes in him will not perish but have eternal
life. God sent his Son into the world not to judge
the world, but to save the world through him.
John 3:16-17

Queen Victoria reigned over the British Empire for almost
sixty-four years.

The Empire reached the ends of the earth under her
leadership and she was possibly the most powerful person
in the world during her reign. And yet, as the famous story
goes, Queen Victoria had a King to whom she bowed:

> One of the chaplains of her late majesty, Queen
> Victoria, had been preaching on the Second
> Coming of the Lord, and afterward, in
> conversation with the preacher, the Queen
> exclaimed: 'Oh! How I wish that the Lord would
> come in my lifetime!' 'Why,' asked the chaplain,

'does your Majesty feel this very earnest desire?'
The Queen replied with quivering lips, and her
whole countenance lighted up by deep emotion
– 'I should so love to lay my crown at His feet.'[57]

Jesus told a parable about two men, one wealthy and the other poor. The wealthy man lived in luxury every day and dressed as royalty. The poor man sat at the gate of the wealthy man's home in the hope that he could live off discarded scraps. This poor man suffered terribly and received little mercy.

The time came when both men died and found themselves in Hades, the Greek word for the Hebrew Sheol, a place the dead were believed to gather awaiting God's exposing judgement. The poor man found himself at Abraham's side – the great father of all who lived with faith, awaiting the paradise we mentioned earlier. But the rich man found himself a long way from Abraham, among the flames, suffering. This is where we pick up the story:

> In Hades, where he was in torment, he looked up and saw Abraham far away, with Lazarus by his side. So he called to him, 'Father Abraham, have pity on me and send Lazarus to dip the tip of his finger in water and cool my tongue, because I am in agony in this fire.'
>
> But Abraham replied, 'Son, remember that in your lifetime you received your good things, while Lazarus received bad things, but now he is comforted here and you are in agony. And

[57] Algernon James Pollock, *The Journey and its End* (Crewe: Scripture Truth Publications, 1990), p113.

besides all this, between us and you a great
chasm has been set in place, so that those who
want to go from here to you cannot, nor can
anyone cross over from there to us.'
Luke 16:23-26 (NIV)

While this was only a story, Jesus was using this method
to teach us a truth about what comes next, and more
importantly, how our lives *here* have influence over *there*.
Let's just observe a few things from this story.

First, the wealthy man finds himself in torment. If we
take it literally, it appears to be both physical (he is
suffering owing to the fire, but not being consumed by it),
and emotional (he has great regret and desperation to
change his circumstances). He is experiencing the very
suffering he ignored at his own gate while alive – that of
being the poor man, with his inability to change his
circumstances despite being in sight of the cure. The same
theme is present throughout all references to life *there*
without God – the *torment of regret and the knowledge of
hopelessness*.

There is some debate about the duration of this
suffering. Beyond Hades and the judgement day, some
scriptures point towards an eternal conscious experience
of suffering in hell, the ultimate destination of
unrepentant souls (for example, see Daniel 12:2; Matthew
25:46; Revelation 14:11). Others sound as if there is an end
to existence (for example, see John 3:16; Matthew 10:28;
Romans 9:22). I won't debate those points of view in this
book, but simply point out that, in either case, it is so bad
in Hades that the wealthy man is desperate to leave it, and

123

following the passage above, desperate to save his living family from it.[58]

Second, only the poor man is named by Jesus. The unnamed wealthy man could represent not only himself, but also everyone who lives for themselves without regard for justice. The naming of poor Lazarus shows that Jesus personally knows those who are His, and that He is attentive to their situation.

Third, it is not possible at this point to change what has already been decided. Abraham and Lazarus are unable to reach the wealthy man with any water owing to the great chasm between them. This tells us that the decisions we make during our lives determine which waiting room we will end up in.

So, to recap, Hades, and anything beyond it, is a place of unimaginable torment; Jesus knows those who are His by name; and the decision to come to Christ for salvation needs to take place *here* before we arrive *there*.

> But remember that [people] will have to face God, who stands ready to judge everyone, both the living and the dead.
> *1 Peter 4:5*

The Bible teaches that all of us are morally accountable to God for our lives. We may, to a degree, get away with many things on earth, but every motive, decision and action will be as clear as the noonday sun when God reveals them on the day that He judges 'the living and the dead'. What hope is there for anyone? How could we

---

[58] See Luke 16:27-31.

remove the weight of wrongs that would so clearly condemn us?

If there is no justification – which means no righting of the wrongs between us and our creator – then we will continue unjustified beyond the grave. Forgiveness has been provided for, but we must acknowledge and receive it in a spirit of repentance. We know this to be true in life. If someone sins against us in a grievous manner, while we are called to forgive, that forgiveness doesn't mean the relationship is restored back to its previous state. We await a response that we hope contains a sincere sense of recognition and apology before we can fully reconcile our relationship. What's true in our human relationships is true with God. Only then, *we* are the ones who need to surrender in humility and acknowledge our need for forgiveness. No amount of money or self-driven effort will change our position or bring about reconciliation. Like the poor man, we must acknowledge our complete lack of ability to solve this on our own, and depend on someone who can. The key to arriving in the right waiting room, then, is in our surrender to Jesus the King, the only one who can forgive and justify us.

It appears that surrender is what Queen Victoria hoped to do, visibly, before Jesus at His return. While this opportunity was not afforded to her, as with Lazarus, Jesus knew the condition of her heart. If she had already surrendered, her name was already known.

Surrendering means coming to terms with our condition before God, for which the Bible has many descriptive terms, such as 'lost', 'blind', 'faithless', hard-hearted, 'dead', 'sinful', wicked and 'rebellious'.[59] While stark, the truth is that if we look within ourselves, we can all identify these conditions running through our veins. This keeps us from everything God has for us *here* and *there*, and above all from a life-giving relationship with Him. Instead of fighting the facts, we are to surrender and accept that we cannot escape accountability or save ourselves.

Surrendering with faith opens the door to complete forgiveness and restoration of our relationship with God. Jesus makes all this possible because He first surrendered His life for us. His death on the cross was in our place. We should have been punished, but He was punished for us.[60] The result is that we can be completely forgiven and freed from the condemnation we deserve.

Surrendering is a choice of our free will. God doesn't force us to respond to this gift, nor does He will for us to go to hell and send us there as if He were mean or vindictive. He creates the path and, like the wealthy man and Queen Victoria, we have the freedom to choose the direction we walk in. Jesus' story reminds us most importantly that we must make the decision *here* before we arrive *there*.

[59] See Luke 19:10; John 9:39; Jeremiah 3:22 (NIV); John 12:40; Ephesians 2:1; Romans 7:5; Romans 1:29; Psalm 25:7.
[60] See Isaiah 53:5.

Take it further

- Are you confident that you have surrendered to Jesus as King of your life, and received His gift of forgiveness?

- While not our main message, the knowledge of hell provides strong motivation for us to share the good news with our neighbour, in the hope of rescuing them from forever without God. We do this by showing and sharing Christ. How urgent does that purpose currently feel? Who do you know that you could begin to pray for? Perhaps you could look for the opportunity and summon the courage to share your faith with them, or to invite them to an Alpha course, or similar?[61]

Take it to Jesus

Jesus, I surrender everything to You. Forgive my many failures and set me free from the guilt of them. Make me right with You once and for all. I lay down at Your feet all the things I've made too important, and choose to surrender to You as Lord of my life today and every day. Help me to experience the presence of Your Spirit, the fullness of Your forgiveness, the depth of Your love and the overwhelming joy of Your hope.
Amen.

---

[61] See www.alpha.org (accessed 25th May 2021).

The reason we're not *there* yet
is because God has an
assignment for each of us *here*.
If billions of souls were not on
the edge of the cliff facing an
eternity without Jesus, we would
already be in paradise, glorified
and chilling. Think about it: the
one and only thing we are not
able to do on the other side is
rescue anyone.

14
What Next?

I am torn between the two: I desire to depart
and be with Christ, which is better by far; but it
is more necessary for you that I remain in the
body. Convinced of this, I know that I will
remain, and I will continue with all of you for
your progress and joy in the faith.
Philippians 1:23-25, NIV

I remember Jesus standing in front of me.

It was the spring of 1996. I was seventeen and I had sneaked into a Christian conference in Bognor Regis without paying. Don't judge, Jesus has forgiven me. One night a guest speaker gave the call to come down to the front and receive prayer if we felt stirred to offer our lives in the service of Jesus Christ. Along with a whole bunch of people, my heart had been grabbed and I sensed the tug of the Holy Spirit, calling me to account for myself there.

As I stood, surrounded by what must have been 100 other young men and women, I felt like I could have been the only one in the room. I vividly remember the moment.

It was as if Jesus walked among us and then stood directly in front of me and reached out His hands to touch me. I knew He was calling me to leave everything and follow Him wherever He led me. It was one of the few unmistakable moments in my life where I have met Him and been entirely undone. It was my calling.

I didn't know what saying yes would mean for me, or where it would take me. I didn't have any qualifications or standout gifts. But I discovered a purpose worth living and dying for and I knew nothing else would satisfy. I had been enlisted and I wanted to know what God wanted me to do next.

We can see in Philippians that Paul had also been enlisted. He was convinced his life on earth was inextricably tied to God's unique purpose for him, and the only thing keeping him from *there*. He longed to be with Christ, but he also knew what God needed him to do *next*: to 'continue with all of you for your progress and joy in the faith'.

Did you catch that?

The reason we're not *there* yet is because God has an assignment for each of us *here*. If billions of souls were not on the edge of the cliff facing an eternity without Jesus, we would already be in paradise, glorified and chilling. Think about it: the one and only thing we are not able to do on the other side is rescue anyone.

So until we get *there*, we have an assignment *here*.

> Surely your goodness and love will follow me
> all the days of my life,
> and I will dwell in the house of the LORD for ever.
> *Psalm 23:6 (NIV)*

Peter is a family man. His wife, three children and five grandchildren love him deeply and will tell you he is a great father and friend. Peter was a medical practitioner for nearly thirty years and, like many of us, worked extremely hard to provide for them. Before his diagnosis, Peter was always active, enjoying things like swimming, walking, gardening and serving his local church.

But at the age of fifty-three, Peter began to notice changes in his body which eventually led him to see a neurologist in 2008. In his own words:[62]

> It started with shaking in my calf muscles. But I was fit and active, so I carried on hoping for the best. However, although I felt well, I lost weight and the muscle shaking worsened. Eventually I saw a neurologist and had tests on my motor nerves. The results pointed to a diagnosis of motor neurone disease.

In January 2012 the diagnosis was confirmed as an atypical slow-moving form of motor neurone disease (MND), for which there is no cure. The next few years became extremely difficult as Peter's condition worsened and his life changed beyond recognition. MND causes a degeneration of the motor nerves (neurones) in the brain and spinal cord that tell the muscles what to do. The result is a weakening and wasting of muscles throughout the body. Peter, so used to being fit and active, succumbed to the disease and all strength began to gradually leave his body:

---

[62] Used with permission.

I was not in a good condition. Within five years I was walking with two sticks and finding myself very breathless. As this worsened, I was told I would need a tracheostomy and eventually moved on to having twenty-four-hour ventilation.

To support his ever-increasing needs, care specialists were brought in around the clock. Bit by bit, Peter's body shut down even basic motor controls that we all take for granted. This is Peter at the time of writing:

I'm unable to swallow and am fed through a tube in my stomach. All my motor nerves have given up so no muscles work, except my eye muscles. Thanks to modern technology I can operate my computer with my eyes. And this is how I keep in contact with the outside world; through texts, emails and the internet.

Under these circumstances, nobody would blame Peter if he were resentful, perhaps bitter, about the cruel suffering he has had to endure, or for giving up faith, and hope, and service to Jesus, but that's not the Peter I know. Not in the slightest.

The faith Peter professed in the light is shining now in the dark. The generosity of his character has been untouched by the loss of his strength. If you had talked with him, as I did, during the last few years, you would have heard joy, gratefulness and encouragement through the electronic speech aid placed on his voice box. Even without this ability now, God is using all he has left – just a blink – to convey messages of life to people around the world. Instead of drowning in an ocean of fear and resentment, hope is enabling Peter to walk on the water in the storm.[63]

Mark 6:56 tells us:

> Wherever [Jesus] went – in villages, cities, or the countryside – they brought the sick out to the marketplaces. They begged him to let the sick touch at least the fringe of his robe, and all who touched him were healed.

Peter writes about this passage:

> What hectic days for Jesus and His disciples. Did they finally hope they would have time to rest? After all, they had now landed and anchored. But as soon as they got out of the boat there was more frantic activity. The people recognised, they ran, they carried, they placed, they begged. Such activity around Jesus. Such power. Such results. Even touching the edge of His cloak brought healing ... I'd be unable to reach out to touch Him. I only have eye movements. And not sure I'd survive being speeded into the marketplace on a mat! But maybe better for me to sit quietly enjoying the presence of Jesus. Knowing the touch of His hand on my life. Reading, meditating, praying, worshipping. And ready to follow the next events Mark has

---

[63] See Matthew 14:25-33.

recorded for us. And whatever God has planned for me.

'And whatever God has planned for me.'

That's inspiring, isn't it? If Peter can ask, 'God, what's next?' after all he has been through, with only his eye muscles left working, then I've got to quit making excuses and start listening, right?

Does Peter ever struggle? Sure. But listen to the grace of God on his journey:

> I never imagined I could get to this level of disability and be content. Of course, I have ups and downs but generally I am at peace. I often recite Psalm 23 from memory during the night. One verse speaks about walking 'through the valley of the shadow of death', and I feel as if I've been going through that valley for a long time. But the verse goes on to say, 'I will fear no evil, for you [God] are with me'.[64] Those are two things I've enjoyed through my motor neurone journey. A lack of fear. And knowing God is with me. I'm not pretending that there are not tough times, but I've known many blessings and expect many more. I believe my present days, however long or short, are in God's hands. My future beyond this earthly life will be with Christ. Revelation 21:4 tells me there will be no more tears or suffering. I look forward to a glorious resurrection body.

---

[64] Psalm 23:4, ESV.

No fear.

A holy presence.

He's faced with unimaginable challenges each day but is filled with 'confident hope'.

He's suffering yet inwardly smiling.

He's believing in the goodness and love of God to follow him both *here* and *there,* whether healed or not, with everything or with nothing. There's something extremely glorious happening *within* him, while on the outside his body crumbles. It's only possible because Peter has in his heart the piece so many are missing in the puzzle of their faith: the 'confident hope' in what's to come.

Now, if God can use Peter's blink, God can use whatever you and I are able to give. All we must do is ask, 'God, before I get *there,* what's *next?*'

God will take us *there* when our assignment is complete, and not a day before. All your days are numbered by Him.[65] Completing your assignment *here* and knowing your priceless inheritance *there* will cause your 'confident hope' to shine in life, and maybe, just maybe, you'll reach the final moments with a beaming smile, just as the lady in the story at the beginning of this book had as she crossed the finishing line. Or, like Stephen, you'll look up and see Jesus in glory. Or, like my friend Peter, you'll walk on water.

Above all, I pray that fear would be replaced by the peace that comes with a deep faith in Jesus, the resurrection, the life, and that you would come to know that the worst-case scenario is the best thing that could happen to you.

---

[65] See Psalm 39:4.

Take it further

- What steps could you take to discover your assignment?

- Considering Peter's story, what excuses might you need to overcome?

Take it to Jesus

Jesus, before I get there, what's next? Help me to discover what You want me to do with my time, my gifts and my opportunities in this season. Like Peter, help me to overcome my obstacles and serve You with everything I have, even if that's only a little. Give me courage to 'fight the good fight'[66] of faith until the day my assignment is complete, and I am rewarded in Your presence with a 'crown of life'.[67]
Amen.

---

[66] 1 Timothy 6:12.
[67] James 1:12.

Recommended Reading

If this book has whetted your appetite to study heaven and other issues in more theological detail, I would recommend the following:

N T Wright, *Surprised by Hope* (San Francisco, CA: HarperOne, 2007).

Randy Alcorn, *Heaven* (Carol Stream, IL: Tyndale House Publishers, 2004).

J Oswald Sanders, *Heaven: Better By Far* (Buckhurst Hill: Billy Graham Evangelistic Association, 1994).

Francis Chan and Preston Sprinkle, *Erasing Hell* (Colorado Springs, CO: David C Cook, 2011).

Rick Warren, *The Purpose Driven Life* (Grand Rapids, MI: Zondervan, 2013).

Wendy Bray and Diana Priest, *Insight into Bereavement* (Farnham: CWR, 2006).

Recommended Websites

If you are interested in exploring the Christian life further:

- For information about the Alpha course:
  www.alpha.org

- 'How to Become a Christian', canonjjohn.com/how-
  to-become-a-christian

If you feel you would like to know more about how to live free in Jesus:

- Freedom in Christ Ministries: ficm.org

For areas around bereavement and other issues that may have been raised for you:

- www.biblesociety.org.uk/what-we-do/england-and-
  wales/funeral-planning-service/dealing-with-
  bereavement/

- www.acc-uk.org/find-a-counsellor/search-for-a-
  counsellor.html

About the Author

Michael is married to Dani and they have a son, Jackson. Michael is part of the leadership team of the One Church Network, within the Assemblies of God, and together Michael and Dani have been the location pastors in Bristol, UK, since 2007.

You can contact the author through his publisher, Instant Apostle: www.instantapostle.com